PRAIS

PRAYING PRODIGALS HOME

A book filled with hope, practical wisdom and encouragement for parents of prodigals—not only to help them let go and wait in peace instead of panic, but to persevere in praying their children home to God's heart.

Cheri Fuller
Author of *When Mothers Pray*
Oklahoma City, Oklahoma

File this one under H for "Hope"! *Praying Prodigals Home* is filled with wise counsel offered with lots of heart. As I considered the timeliness of this work in the big picture, it occurs to me that in the matter of the great end-time falling away referred to in Scripture, there can be—and will be through persevering, hope-filled prayer—a great return!

Esther Ilnisky
Author of *Let the Children Pray*
West Palm Beach, Florida

There is no pain like that of having a prodigal in your life.
I have experienced this personally, and I have seen a great victory.
I only wish I had had this book to read during the times when it seemed like nothing would ever change in my child's life.
This book will comfort you and give you hope.

Cindy Jacobs
Cofounder, Generals of Intercession
Colorado Springs, Colorado

Praying Prodigals Home is great encouragement and guidance for believers who grieve over and pray for wandering loved ones.

Dee Jepsen
Author of *Jesus Called Her Mother*
President Emeritus, Enough Is Enough
Port Charles, Florida

Praying Prodigals Home will give you (1) hope when you feel hopeless, (2) insights when you can't figure out or fix anymore and (3) direction when you feel tossed about by your prodigal's ways. The only question left unanswered at the end of this book is "How long?" I'm waiting, too, for my prodigal to come home. Let's take these tools, dear friend, and go the distance.

Miriam Neff
Author and counselor
Kildeer, Illinois

This pragmatic book faces tough issues and provides answers based on solid spiritual truths. A worthy read!

Morris L. Sheats
Senior Pastor, Hillcrest Church
Dallas, Texas

Some books about pain remain aloof from the agony, promising help for the hurting but often delivering little more than irritating recipes from unsaved theoreticians. Others are so saturated in hurt that they serve to sympathize but offer scant hope. *Praying Prodigals Home* is a ray of light from two women who have waded through the corporeal darkness known only to the parents of prodigal children. Real and frank but with a merciful river of joy and faith, this book comforts those who sit in fear while their loved ones trek through the far country. The writers beckon us to reach beyond the pain to a higher plateau, where something called peace is to be had, even amidst the grief.

Mark Rutland
President, Southeastern College
Lakeland, Florida

Your prodigals may have moved to a far country but rest assured, God has their address. *Praying Prodigals Home* reminds us that He can and will save them. This book is a faith builder!

Thetus Tenney
Author of *Prayer Takes Wings*
Tioga, Louisiana

From the heart of these two mothers has come wise counsel. You can tell that they've been listening to the Father! This book is filled with story after story, all of them pregnant with hope. As I read this manuscript on an airplane, hot tears filled my eyes and high hope filled my heart. I had to set the pages aside and spend a few minutes praying for my three daughters from seat 4A at 30,000 feet. Thank you, Quin Sherrer and Ruthanne Garlock, for helping us pray with understanding! I plan to give this book to several close friends and relatives. It's like sowing seeds of hope.

Tommy Tenney
Author of *The God Chasers* and *God's Dream Team*
Pineville, Louisiana

This book is a must! Quin Sherrer and Ruthanne Garlock have filled it with testimonies that act as a spoon with which to stir your faith. These are not stories of "spooky" happenings that frightened backsliders back to God but, rather, of God's miraculous intervention in answer to prayers. This is a beautiful portrait of a supernatural God working in the natural to draw to Himself our loved ones who are lost. I highly recommend that you read *Praying Prodigals Home* and that you keep an extra copy around to give to someone whose faith needs bolstering.

Iverna Tompkins
Conference speaker
Phoenix, Arizona

Here are amazingly powerful testimonies of believers who have prayed back home beloved prodigals, ages 15 to 94. Loaded with pearls like "Pride is a luxury parents can't afford when wooing their child back from the pit," this book is filled with unforgettable stories from well-known and unknown parents who have stood in the gap for a prodigal.

Marion Bond West
Author and Contributing Editor, *Guideposts*
Watkinsville, Georgia

PRAYING PRODIGALS HOME

QUIN SHERRER
AND
RUTHANNE GARLOCK

Regal

A Division of Gospel Light
Ventura, California, U.S.A.

Published by Regal Books
A Division of Gospel Light
Ventura, California, U.S.A.
Printed in U.S.A.

Regal Books is a ministry of Gospel Light, an evangelical Christian publisher dedicated to serving the local church. We believe God's vision for Gospel Light is to provide church leaders with biblical, user-friendly materials that will help them evangelize, disciple and minister to children, youth and families.

It is our prayer that this Regal book will help you discover biblical truth for your own life and help you meet the needs of others. May God richly bless you.

For a free catalog of resources from Regal Books and Gospel Light, please call your Christian supplier or contact us at 1-800-4-GOSPEL *or* www.regalbooks.com.

The stories shared here are real, but details of certain events and names of individuals and locations mentioned have been changed to protect the privacy of the persons involved, and to maintain confidentiality. Any similarity between persons in this book and individuals known to the reader is strictly coincidental.

Cover Design by Barbara LeVan Fisher
Interior Design by Rob Williams
Edited by Deena Davis

Library of Congress Cataloging-in-Publication Data
Sherrer, Quin.
    Praying prodigals home / Quin Sherrer and Ruthanne Garlock.
        p. cm.
    Includes bibliographical references.
    ISBN 0-8307-2563-6
    1. Intercessory prayer—Christianity. 2. Parents—Religious life. I. Garlock, Ruthanne.
    II. Title.

BV210.2 .S5147 2000
248.3'2—dc21   00-032327

1 2 3 4 5 6 7 8 9 10 11 12 13 14 15 / 07 06 05 04 03 02 01 00

Rights for publishing this book in other languages are contracted by Gospel Literature International (GLINT). GLINT also provides technical help for the adaptation, translation and publishing of Bible study resources and books in scores of languages worldwide. For further information, write to GLINT, P.O. Box 4060, Ontario, CA 91761-1003, U.S.A. You may also send e-mail to Glintint@aol.com, or visit the GLINT website at www.glint.org.

CONTENTS

Having suffered great disillusionment and emotional pain, a young man who had once known God found himself confused, disoriented and away from his Father's house.

"It seemed strange," he would later testify, "to find myself in a drunken state or a drug-induced high, rejecting the God of my childhood and youth. A part of me still loved and wanted God and believed His ways were right, while another part of me seemed unable to find my way out of the fog.

"On several occasions, I remember the Holy Spirit's clear and quiet voice making itself heard over the clamor of loud music and marijuana-dulled senses. 'Why are you doing this?' (I knew the question was for me, not Him. He already knew very well my confusion.) 'You know this isn't who you really are. You belong to Me, and I won't let you go,' the Holy Spirit would gently remind me. It amazed me that He would pursue me in such places.

"At times I would leave the bar and walk for a while, high on drugs, yet communing with the God who wouldn't let me go. For a season I continued to blindly run the maze of my confused condition, crashing into pain after pain and disillusionment after disillusionment.

"Then one day, the not-to-be-denied love of God caught up with me and crashed through all my fears and facades. Another prodigal came to his senses, finding himself in the loving embrace of a heavenly Father whose determined love was greater than Satan's determined hatred and seemingly indestructible hold."

I know the young man of this story well. I can fill in all the gaps and read between all the lines. I understand his confusion,

I can identify with his pain, and I know the overwhelming power of the love and grace of God that he experienced. I know these things because I was that young man.

That's why I'm so excited about this book. I believe in the hope it will birth in thousands of people. It is a book of hope for the weary, worn-out, interceding warrior who struggles to keep believing. It is a book of hope for the brokenhearted parent who has asked a thousand times, through a million condemning tears, "What did I do wrong?"

It is a book that will not only produce comforting hope, but it also will leave the reader with a clear and confident strategy of prevailing prayer and effective action.

I believe God is greater than rebellion.

I believe the Father's love is stronger than the prodigal's pain.

I believe the Holy Spirit can run down any fleeing family member.

I believe the sword of the Spirit is sharper and more powerful than the sting of the serpent.

I believe the dormant seeds of truth—though asleep as in winter—will one day break through the soil of deception and produce the fruit of life.

I believe in the power of prayer.

And I believe the prodigals are coming home!

Read this book. It was written for you. As you read, you will laugh, cry, pray and rejoice. But most all, you will walk away from it with a renewed faith in the Father and hope for the prodigal. Your prayers will be empowered, your faith will be renewed and, ultimately, your broken heart will be healed.

Thank you, Quin and Ruthanne, for this invaluable gift to believers everywhere. It will unquestionably bear much fruit. But I think the biggest thank-you comes from the heavenly Father who is going to use this book to bring many thousands of prodigals back into His loving embrace.

May His pleasure be your greatest reward!

Dutch Sheets
Colorado Springs, CO

ACKNOWLEDGMENTS

Special thanks to:

Billie Baptiste of Regal Books, who came up with the topic of this book; Doris Greig, wife of Gospel Light's chairman, who was our cheerleader from the first time she heard the title; Bill Greig III, Kyle Duncan and Deena Davis of Regal, who believed in the book and helped it through the publishing process.

Pastor Peter Lord of Titusville, Florida, who prayed with us (Quin and LeRoy) for our youngsters during their difficult years, and who taught us much by his own example as he prayed and believed for his own prodigals.

My husband, LeRoy, and children, Quinett, Keith and Sherry, for their constant support and prayer for this book.

I am extremely grateful to John Garlock for allowing Ruthanne and me days of writing time at "Angelwing," their lovely log home in the Texas hill country. His intense prayers and advice were special.

An extraordinary thanks to the women and men who shared with us stories of their own struggles for prodigals. Without them this book could not have been written. To our intercessors who stood in prayer with us through every phase of this project—may God reward you.

And to our Lord Jesus Christ—who always causes us to triumph—be honor and glory and praise forever. Amen.

—Quin Sherrer

Prodigals in your family.

Never had them? Then thank God, and pray for your friends who do.

All three of my youngsters were prodigals. But God taught my husband, LeRoy, and me many valuable lessons in praying them out of the enemy's camp and back into God's kingdom. Because of those lessons, we can offer hope to those still praying, believing and waiting for their prodigals to repent—whether they are children, parents, siblings or aunts and uncles.

Just today I read again the Scripture posted beside my bed: "But with God all things are possible" (Matt. 19:26). That verse sustained me time and again when my faith waned.

When we began our prayer venture for our prodigals, not much was written on how to pray for those who had turned their backs on God's plans and purposes for their lives. That led us to search the Scriptures and ask the Holy Spirit to teach us. And it drew LeRoy and me to pray together daily in agreement for our children and their friends. Today, all are serving God—and together we are standing in the prayer gap for five little ones (our grandchildren), ranging in age from two to five.

"The prodigals are coming home in droves," our pastor, Dutch Sheets, announced at the turn of the year. And it's happening. In recent months, relatives we've prayed for over many years have made a turnaround and have returned to the God of their youth.

During the time we were praying for our own prodigals, I read and reread Jesus' parable of the prodigal son (see Luke 15). I also learned that in the seventeenth century, the Dutch artist Rembrandt had done an oil painting that depicted this well-known story. I longed to see it, but it was tucked away among thousands of artifacts in the Hermitage Museum in St. Petersburg, Russia.

Just a few years ago, I found myself at the Hermitage, standing transfixed as I studied *The Return of the Prodigal Son*. Eight feet high by six feet wide, the huge painting is of a father embracing his son who has just come home. With strong hands resting on the shoulders of the kneeling, rag-clad young man, the father is the focal point. The natural light of the large nearby window heightens the stunning contrast of colors—dark background, abundant reds, browns and touches of yellow.

Tears clouded my vision as I studied the father's countenance. It seemed God Himself was giving me a personal, reassuring message. *I love you even more than this father loves his beloved son who was lost,* God spoke to my heart. *I long to welcome home so many more of My prodigals.* I immediately sensed a new commission to pray more fervently for those who don't know God as their loving heavenly Father.

Every time I see a print of this painting, I am again drawn to the love in the father's eyes. Maybe your experience is like mine: You can *never* remember a time when your father put his arm about your shoulders or gave you gifts or set a table in your honor or welcomed you home. But God, our *heavenly* Father—always with open arms—wants to welcome us or anyone who will accept His love and embrace.

When the prodigals you are praying for return, what a "Welcome home!" celebration you can throw. Remember, the battle is the Lord's. He is the one who is calling them home. We simply align our prayers with His will and purpose.

I pray that this book, a companion to *How to Pray for Your Children*, will encourage and challenge you to never stop praying. As you read stories of other intercessors who share their defeats, victories, strategies, hopes and promises from God for their one-time prodigals, may you be inspired to believe and expect your own miracle, too.

—Quin Sherrer

Story of the Lost Son

A man had two sons. The younger son told his father, "I want my share of your estate now, instead of waiting until you die." So his father agreed to divide his wealth between his sons.

A few days later this younger son packed all his belongings and took a trip to a distant land, and there he wasted all his money on wild living. About the time his money ran out, a great famine swept over the land, and he began to starve. He persuaded a local farmer to hire him to feed his pigs. The boy became so hungry that even the pods he was feeding the pigs looked good to him. But no one gave him anything.

When he finally came to his senses, he said to himself, "At home even the hired men have food enough to spare, and here I am, dying of hunger! I will go home to my father and say, 'Father, I have sinned against both heaven and you, and I am no longer worthy of being called your son. Please take me on as a hired man.'"

So he returned home to his father. And while he was still a long distance away, his father saw him coming. Filled with love and compassion, he ran to his son, embraced him, and kissed him. His son said to him, "Father, I have sinned against both heaven and you, and I am no longer worthy of being called your son."

But his father said to the servants, "Quick! Bring the finest robe in the house and put it on him. Get a ring for his finger, and sandals for his feet. And kill the calf we have been fattening in the pen. We must celebrate with a feast, for this son of mine was dead and has now returned to life. He was lost, but now he is found." So the party began.

Meanwhile, the older son was in the fields working. When he returned home, he heard music and dancing in the house, and he asked one of the servants what was going on. "Your brother is back," he was told, "and your father has killed the calf we were fattening and has prepared a great feast. We are celebrating because of his safe return."

The older brother was angry and wouldn't go in. His father came out and begged him, but he replied, "All these years I've worked hard for you and never once refused to do a single thing you told me to. And in all that time you never gave me even one young goat for a feast with my friends. Yet when this son of yours comes back after squandering your money on prostitutes you celebrate by killing the finest calf we have."

His father said to him, "Look, dear son, you and I are very close, and everything I have is yours. We had to celebrate this happy day. For your brother was dead and has come back to life! He was lost, but now he is found!"

—Luke 15:11-32, *NLT*

CHAPTER ONE

The Making of a Prodigal

The younger son got together all he had, set off for a distant country and there squandered his wealth in wild living.

—LUKE 15:13

The story of the prodigal son is the story of a God who goes searching for me and who doesn't rest until he has found me. He urges and he pleads. He begs me to stop clinging to the powers of death and to let myself be embraced by arms that will carry me to the place where I will find the life I most desire.[1]

—HENRI J. M. NOUWEN

If you are a parent praying for a prodigal son or daughter, you know the anguish that comes with watching a child you deeply care about wander away from God's love. But have you ever stopped to consider God's heartache over His prodigal children?

Adam and Eve, the children Father God first created, disobeyed Him—choosing to believe the lie of the serpent over the truth He had given them. Then the nation of Israel, God's chosen people, disappointed Him in the same way. Jesus was betrayed by Judas; Paul was forsaken by Demas. Throughout Scripture we see God's concern for prodigals and His efforts to woo them back.

What about present-day prodigals? We have heard from many parents who not only face the heartbreak caused by a prodigal child, but the agony of making difficult decisions about how to deal with the crisis. For example:

- A 16-year-old daughter is pregnant, and the parents can't agree on whether to allow her to get an abortion.

- A prodigal son returns home unrepentant and a short time later brings his new girlfriend home, expecting that she can spend the night with him.

- A young woman strays from her Christian upbringing, gets caught up in a career in which she makes lots of money, then ends up in prison on charges of fraud.

- The son of a missionary struggles with same-sex attractions after he's molested by a stranger he thought was befriending him. He is a prodigal for several years before he's able to break free.

• Devoted parents of a talented young daughter discover
she's addicted to drugs at age 15. They practice tough
love by putting her in a strictly disciplined rehab program, and she comes out drug-free.

Of course, every prodigal is accountable for his or her wrong
choice to rebel and run away from God. But the underlying
problem of all prodigals is that they don't perceive God as a loving, benevolent heavenly Father. Because of their distorted view
of God, they often are embittered toward Him, blaming Him for
most of their problems. Satan deceived Eve in the garden by con-
vincing her that God was not trustworthy. Deception remains
Satan's most effective tactic today, as evidenced by the enor-
mous number of prodigals whose names fill our prayer lists.

The Aftermath of Abuse

Does the enemy especially target certain children? Often it
appears so. Ministers' children and those with a strong sense of
God's call on their lives at an early age are particularly vulnerable.

Joyce's daughter Alicia is an example of this. Alicia accepted
Jesus as her Savior when she was only three years old and was the
perfect picture of childhood—free, innocent, spontaneous. As
she grew up, it was evident she was gifted in music, art and
dance. She seemed to add a special mark of beauty to everything
she touched. But she was so strong willed that it led to power
struggles with her father from an early age.

"My husband was a powder keg of anger because of his own
poor upbringing, and he never related well to Alicia," Joyce said.

"He abused her verbally and emotionally. Sometimes she said she hated him, but then she took on his ways of venting anger and rage at the least little upset. We divorced when Alicia was 10 years old. I've always known she has a special call upon her life, and we always were very close. But at 13 she began resisting the things of the Lord and turned against me. This was the beginning of her prodigal journey—marked by verbal tirades, swearing, physical outbursts of anger and drinking. At one point she was hospitalized for suicidal tendencies."

When she was 16, a youth pastor sexually abused Alicia, and shortly thereafter two other men did the same thing. She related more easily to boys than to girls but felt they were only interested in her for sex—so she felt isolated, angry and afraid.

From age 17 to 20, Alicia threw caution to the wind and became sexually promiscuous. Though she never totally turned her back on God, she was angry with Him, feeling He had failed to protect her from being abused. Joyce insisted that Alicia see a Christian counselor, who helped her find more appropriate ways to express her hostility. But her behavior didn't change.

At age 20, when her sexual promiscuity was at its peak, Alicia went to a doctor on her own because of troubling symptoms that scared her. After tests, the doctor called her with a very bad report, saying she needed to come in for more tests. That wake-up call devastated Alicia. Afraid her life might be cut short, she now saw her mom as her friend and advocate, not her enemy, and asked her to call her prayer partners to pray.

"My friends and I had prayed for years for this rebel to renounce her anger and for God to reveal His love to her," Joyce said. "This health crisis was the turning point. A few weeks later I went with her when she had two painful diagnostic procedures to pinpoint the problem more specifically. Amazingly, this time the tests came back with a good report—'Nothing is wrong,' the nurse assured her. 'Just come back in six months for a checkup.'

"We are convinced that God supernaturally healed Alicia of this disease. After experiencing His incredible mercy and grace, at last she saw God differently—as a Father who loved her in spite of her rebellion. She broke off all ungodly relationships, began reading the Word and asking me to read with her; now she attends church consistently. She is *living* this change of heart and treating me with respect and affection. Also, she has forgiven her father and all the men in her life whom she felt had used her and disappointed her. Recently she bought a ring to wear as a reminder of her pledge—'No sex until I marry.' "

Of course, every prodigal is responsible for his or her choices. We don't believe God inflicted symptoms of a serious illness on Alicia just because she was so rebellious. But He did allow these things to happen—all the while calling her to turn her heart toward Him.

God's Arms Are Always Extended

What does the word "prodigal" mean to you? The word—based on the Latin word *prodigus,* meaning "wasteful" or "extravagant"—does not appear in Scripture. It describes the younger son's behavior, and thus the story came to be called The Parable of the Prodigal Son. But it could more accurately be called The Parable of the Lost Son.

The story is the final and longest segment of a three-part parable in which Jesus describes the lost sheep, the lost coin and the lost son. The sheep was lost because of its aimless wandering. The coin was lost within the house through the carelessness or preoccupation of its owner. But the son, who willfully inflicted deep sorrow upon his father, was lost because of his own conscious and deliberate action.

How many of us, at one time or another, have held a distorted picture of God's love?

Each vignette clearly communicates God's desire to "seek and to save what was lost" (Luke 19:10). Jesus is depicted as the shepherd who seeks and finds the lost sheep, the woman who searches and finds the lost coin, and the father who rejoices when his lost son returns home. Jesus tells the parable in response to the Pharisees' complaint that He "welcomes sinners and eats with them" (Luke 15:2). While these religious leaders were intent on chastising sinners, Jesus' purpose was—and still is—to redeem them.

How many of us, at one time or another, have held a distorted picture of God's love? Author Philip Yancey reveals that in his own legalistic upbringing his concept of what grace really means didn't fit with this parable:

How different are these stories from my own childhood notions about God: a God who forgives, yes, but reluctantly, after making the penitent squirm. I imagined God as a distant thundering figure who prefers fear and respect to love. Jesus tells instead of a father publicly humiliating himself by rushing out to embrace a son who has squandered half the family fortune. There is no solemn lecture, "I hope you've learned your lesson!" Instead, Jesus tells of the father's exhilaration— "This my son was dead, and is alive again; he was lost, and is found"—and then adds the buoyant phrase, "they began to make merry."

What blocks forgiveness is not God's reticence . . . but ours. God's arms are always extended; we are the ones who turn away. . . .

A housewife jumping up and down in glee over the discovery of a lost coin is not what naturally comes to mind when I think of God. Yet that is the image Jesus insisted upon. [2]

What Produces a Prodigal?

Of all the parables Jesus told, the story of the prodigal son is among the most widely known. Even secular writers use the term in referring to a person who abandons the values of his upbringing to pursue a reckless, wanton lifestyle.

In the biblical account, the father does not seem to be a deficient parent. But at least three elements influenced the younger son:

His *impatience*—he was not willing to wait for his inheritance.

His *selfishness*—he was more interested in himself than in honoring his father.

His *desire for adventure*—the far country was more exciting than the family homestead.

Recently we had lunch with Terry, a friend who shared the struggles she's had with her prodigal son, Jason. He grew up loving the Lord, but in high school he got involved with a skinhead gang. As a result of much prayer he left the gang, but his life was in danger when gang members threatened retaliation. For several weeks he lived with friends in another city. Hoping to get his life on track, he enrolled in Bible school, but soon he was kicked out for smoking and he moved home again.

"So, how's he doing now?" we asked.

"Well, he's supposed to be looking for a job, but it's hard because he never finished high school or his equivalency test," she told us. "He has a bright orange Mohawk haircut, hangs out with guys at a pool hall and sometimes brings one of those guys home with him. Recently I was agitated that he stayed up all night in his room with a friend, but he told me the next day he'd led the boy to the Lord. He comes to church with his orange hair, multiple earrings, and chains and padlock around his neck, almost as a challenge to see how people will receive him. It's amazing what a positive effect it has when someone welcomes him with a hug.

"He complains about inconsistencies in the church. But I said to him, 'Jason, I keep loving you and trying to help you, yet you continually disobey and dishonor me. So who's the hypocrite?' "

Terry is trusting God day by day to give her wisdom in dealing with Jason. She has given him a deadline for getting a job and has offered to help him buy a car so he can drive to work. But she will only match the amount of money he saves.

"I know he's called to be a leader," she said, "but the enemy has deceived him in many areas. I've learned the importance of praying the Word of God over him instead of just 'praying the problem.' I'm confident that he will fulfill the destiny God has for him."

As Jason's story illustrates, an unwillingness to accept any form of authority is a common trait that leads to rebellion. From the profusion of contemporary prodigal stories people have shared with us, we've compiled a list of some of the factors that contribute to their leaving:

- False expectations from parents and/or extended family
- Parents' failure to keep their promises to the child
- Absent, cruel or disinterested fathers
- The hypocrisy of parents and/or the church community
- Feeling their spiritual needs are not met by the church
- Anger at injustices they see in family, church, community or civil government
- A sense of rejection
- The trauma of divorce
- Low self-esteem and a sense of inadequacy
- Sibling rivalry
- Peer pressure
- Lack of acceptance by peers
- Poverty (perceived or real)
- Inattentive, workaholic parents—especially the father
- Desire for doing their own thing, without parental restrictions
- Childhood abuse (emotional, physical or sexual)
- Addictions of all types (pornography, gambling, drinking, drugs, sex, etc.)

Encouraging Research

No matter how hopeless your prodigal situation may seem, the good news is that rebels with a strong Christian background usually return to it at some point in their lives. Research on this subject is limited, but Dr. James Dobson, founder of Focus on the Family, conducted a survey of 35,000 parents regarding their children's acceptance of the Christian values with which they had been raised. He reports:

As can be observed, 53 percent of even the most strong-willed and rebellious children eventually return to the values of their parents, outright. When that figure is combined with those who are "somewhat" accepting of parental perspectives, that means 85 percent of these hardheaded, independent individuals will eventually lean toward their parents' point of view by the time adolescence is over. Only 15 percent are so headstrong that they reject everything their family stood for, and I'll wager that there were other problems and sources of pain in most of those cases.

What this means, in effect, is that these tough-minded kids will fuss and fight and complain throughout their years at home, but the majority will turn around as young adults and do what their parents most desired. . . . If we could evaluate these individuals at thirty-five instead of twenty-four years of age, even fewer would still be in rebellion against parental values.[3]

Tom Bisset, a Christian radio broadcaster, took on the task of interviewing a wide variety of people who had become "faith dropouts." Some of them had returned to the faith; a few were still wandering. But from his study, Mr. Bisset came up with these four major reasons why Christian kids leave the faith:

1. They have troubling, unanswered questions about their faith. . . . Unwilling to "just believe," they opt for "intellectual honesty." To do this they believe they must leave their childhood faith behind in order to find real answers in the real world.
2. Their faith isn't working for them. . . . Disillusioned with the church and their fellow Christians, and ulti-

mately disappointed with God . . . they leave by default; they simply can't do it anymore.

3. Other things in life become more important than their faith. . . . Preoccupied by business, pleasure, material ambitions, personal problems or other hard realities . . . their faith, which was once primary, becomes secondary.

4. They never personally owned their own faith. . . . When these well-meaning but robot-like practitioners of Christianity were faced with a life-shattering experience or other crisis of faith, they did not know what they believed, or if they believed at all.[4]

In Mr. Bisset's interviews with returned prodigals, many of the prodigals told him the strong faith of their parents was part of what drew them back. One said, "Those two things, love and truth, coming together in my parents, modeled God for me. I'm sure it was a part of the reason I came back to my faith." Another said, "Whatever happens in your life, when you're raised in a Christian home, you've got God's truth in here. Eventually it surfaces and pulls you back. You actually want it."[5]

Potential Prodigal

Abram, a 17-year-old now studying welding in a vocational school, is an example of a potential prodigal who turned around when he realized he was headed for big-time trouble. Raised by godly, praying parents, he knew he had little chance of getting by much longer with his rebellion. He was a very adept shoplifter from the sixth to ninth grades.

"It was cool to steal—everybody I knew did it. We'd go into a convenience store and buy one candy bar. Then we'd stash candy in our clothing, go out behind the store and eat it while we planned the next place to hit. It was like an addiction."

In the ninth grade, when he came home with a very expensive pair of sunglasses, his parents got suspicious and confronted him. Later he and some friends climbed up on top of a vacant bank building and began to explore. A security guard—believing they were about to spray-paint graffiti on the walls—caught them and called the police. While driving them to the station, the policeman lectured them and put fear into those boys. However, he was merciful and didn't file charges, though two of the boys had hunting knives on them.

Abram counts that policeman's lecture and the one he'd gotten from his parents earlier about the stolen sunglasses as his wake-up call. "I always knew my parents loved me unconditionally and I didn't want to disappoint them," he said. "And I had a teacher who helped with my assignments after school and sometimes would come to my house on Saturday to tutor me. In turn I would haul hay for her horses. She believed in me, and I didn't want to disappoint her, either."

Abram never sees his old friends since he transferred to another school. Now he and his new friends get together for prayer meetings instead of stealing escapades. Prayer and unconditional love helped turn a potential prodigal into a young man who wants to serve God wholeheartedly.

Poverty Made Her Vulnerable

Barbara is a mother who suffered years of deception and abuse from her husband before the marriage ended in divorce. This caused her to lose her home and most of her possessions, but it also damaged her relationship with her teenage daughter, Carlyn. She and Carlyn then moved to another state to start over.

"After the move, I began attending a Monday-night prayer group and entered into years of intercession for my daughter," Barbara said. "Carlyn despised me, blaming me for the poverty we suffered, and she hated the church. She graduated from high school early and then ran off to Canada to become a model."

In Canada she took up with Robert, a wealthy playboy who talked her into going with him to Europe and around the world, promising connections for her modeling career. He even hinted at the possibility of marriage.

"Carlyn was a prodigal by choice, as she pursued the lifestyle of the rich and the famous," Barbara said. "She lived in France and had her own helicopter for traveling from town to town. She did leave Robert once, but then she let him talk her into rejoining him. After this, Carlyn began calling me from England, Ireland, France—several other places in Europe—begging us to pray for her. Robert had become addicted to cocaine and was beating her. She had no one to call on for help, as he was paying off the hotel staff and the police. He took everything away from her and was literally holding her captive."

For months, Barbara's new husband and her intercessory prayer group joined her in the prayer battle for Carlyn. The frantic phone calls continued.

"I wept many tears over my lost daughter, so afraid of what might happen to her," Barbara said. "About this time, Ruthanne Garlock visited our prayer group one night. She prayed in agreement with me for Carlyn to be delivered and encouraged me to not give up. A short time later when my daughter called, God led me to tell her to sell her jewelry, if necessary, to get some money in order to run away."

Carlyn did that, but Robert caught her and beat her violently. He bribed the police to threaten her, and then notified airports that she was a drug smuggler and should be stopped if she tried to leave. But through many miracles, God enabled Carlyn to escape. Robert and his agents simply lost track of her, and she was able to fly to Chicago.

"She suffered terrible persecution at the airport as the authorities thought she was a drug dealer," her mother said. "But when they could find no evidence, they had to let her go. Those prayers and tears delivered my child back to me after years of abuse. Though Carlyn hasn't yet fully committed her life to God, she knows her freedom is a miracle. Now she has an office job, teaches modeling part-time and is living in our home instead of a mansion in France. Her living with us is a huge miracle, because we have so little by the world's standard. God is surely moving, and I know it's only a matter of time before Carlyn turns back to her heavenly Father with her whole heart. I will never stop praying and fighting for her."

The enemy has many strategies to make prodigals of God's children. But instead of allowing shock and hopelessness to overcome us when they run away, we can retaliate with prayer strategies to reclaim them and draw them home.

Fruitfulness out of Desolation

In some cases, traumatic experiences can so overwhelm young people that their faith in God suffers a tremendous setback. Sixteen-year-old Sam is an example. His mother wrote this account of the events leading to her son's becoming a prodigal:

One evening, Sam and I prayed together as we left the house to go to his high school rodeo. Sam's horse was acting very bizarre that night and broke away from Sam while he was taking the rope off. He galloped all the way to the highway with Sam running behind him. Horrified, Sam watched helplessly as the horse charged into the path of a car.

The young man driving could not avoid hitting the horse. The driver's girlfriend, Sabrina, died on the roadside with Sam kneeling on one side of her and her boyfriend on the other. I prayed with Sabrina's mother at the scene of the accident. They were a strong Christian family and did not press charges. But in the months following, Sam could not handle the catastrophe. Angry at God, he turned to drugs.

Several years before, God had spoken to me through Isaiah 55:13,14: "Instead of the thornbush will grow the pine tree, and instead of briers the myrtle will grow. This will be for the LORD's renown." At the time, I didn't understand what it meant. But now I realized we had to trust God to bring fruitfulness out of this place of desolation in Sam's life. Other prophetic words had been spoken over Sam that we now had to accept by faith.

By fall, a few months after the accident, we knew Sam was failing at school, suicidal, and he was pushing us out of his life. In the spring, school officials initiated a confrontation with our son about the drugs. We worked with counselors and stood up to Sam in the day-to-day battles, as God led us.

Spiritually, we stood on the promises God had given us and spoke them daily. We prayed over the place where Sam's truck is parked and over his room, placing anointed prayer cloths in it. No matter what Sam did (and he did plenty) we spoke what God said about him, and we prayed protection over him and everyone he came in contact with.

For a year and a half it seemed God was silent. One day when I was crying out to Him, I asked, "Lord, why won't You speak to me?"

He said, *I've given you all you need to fight—stand on it.*

Sometimes I would cry and my husband would speak aloud God's words over our son; some days we did it the other way around. But we never went to the bottom together. Several times I thought, *I can't go on.* Then our pastor's wife would be there, shore me up and have me say to the Lord, "I trust You." Those words alone brought us through the darkest times.

No way could we understand or accept the wreck, the loss or the drugs. We simply had to trust God and His promises without question.

About two years after the accident, Sam realized he could not graduate from high school and do drugs. When he started pulling away from drugs, his healing began. About a year later he put flowers on Sabrina's grave and we had a wonderful visit with the family. When the two families prayed for one another, it seemed to bring some closure to the tragedy. Sam is drug free today and continues to be healed as his walk with the Lord grows stronger. And yes, his testimony is bringing praise and glory to God.

Judson Cornwall says this about God's role as our Father:

> Like the prodigal son, those who leave the Father's home are soon abandoned, forsaken, rejected, and ruined, and what seemed like the right way has as its end the ways of death. . . . The prodigal found mercy in the heart of the father when he returned, and so has every other fugitive son of the Father; no returning runaway has ever been rejected, or ever will be. The problem is not the forgiveness and acceptance of the Father, for

that has been vouchsafed by promise, but the intricacy of the return is learning to accept ourselves so that we can walk as His children in love. He is the Father to the runaways.[6]

No matter what disappointment or trauma may have led to your prodigal's situation, God's love will never stop calling him or her home. God shares your heartache and offers comfort and peace as you place your trust in Him.

Prayer

Lord, help me to not dwell on all the negatives I see. Give me Your strength to cross over from feeling helpless to believing You are able and willing to intervene in _____'s life. Forgive me for the wrong things I've said or done that only added to the problem. Show me how I can extend love and forgiveness to _____ and pray more effectively. Thank You, Lord, for Your comfort. Amen.

Questions to Think About

1. Can I identify the factors contributing to my loved one's becoming a prodigal?
2. Have I asked God to forgive me for ways I may have contributed to his/her leaving?

Notes

1. Henri J. M. Nouwen, *The Return of the Prodigal Son* (New York: Doubleday, Image Books, 1992), p. 82.
2. Taken from *What's So Amazing About Grace?* by Philip Yancey. Copyright © 1997 by Philip D. Yancey. Used by permission of Zondervan Publishing House, pp. 46, 47.
3. Dr. James C. Dobson, *Parenting Isn't for Cowards* (Dallas: Word Publishing, 1987), p. 42.
4. Tom Bisset, *Why Christian Kids Leave the Faith* (Nashville: Thomas Nelson, n.d.; Grand Rapids, MI: Discovery House, 1992), pp. 22, 23.
5. Ibid., pp. 158, 191.
6. Judson Cornwall, *Let God Arise* (Old Tappan, NJ: Fleming H. Revell, 1982), pp. 30, 31.

CHAPTER TWO

Prayer Strategies

*In everything, by prayer and petition, with thanksgiving,
present your requests to God. And the peace of God, which
transcends all understanding, will guard your hearts
and your minds in Christ Jesus.*

—PHILIPPIANS 4:6,7

*Someone has said that it is both a wonderful and terrible thing to
be the child of praying parents. To be out of God's will and have
their prayers rising to the Father's house daily on your behalf is to
invite unpredictable consequences.*[1]

—TOM BISSET

When it comes to prayer strategies, the Holy Spirit is wonderfully creative in giving specific guidance. After all, God knows every intimate detail about your prodigal, and He knows exactly the prayer strategy needed to turn that person around. But it does require persistence and patience as you, the prayer warrior, wait on the Lord for His direction.

Intercession—meaning "to stand between"—finds us standing between God and the one for whom we are praying as we ask God to intervene. It also means standing between Satan and the prayer subject, pushing back the spirits of darkness that keep him or her from understanding the truth.

Among the most poignant words in Scripture is God's statement, "I looked for a man among them who would build up the wall and stand before me in the gap on behalf of the land . . . but I found none" (Ezek. 22:30). His cry was for someone to pray against the sin of the nation. His desire today is that we pray and intercede on behalf of those who are alienated from Him.

Intercessors who have used varied approaches to pray for prodigals have shared some of their strategies with us. While not all approaches will apply to your situation, perhaps one or more will provide a biblical springboard for you to consider as the Holy Spirit leads you.

Focused, Compassionate Prayer

One mother said she prays for God to bless her wayward son's business ventures, based on this verse: "Do you despise the riches of His goodness, forbearance, and longsuffering, not knowing that the goodness of God leads you to repentance?" (Rom. 2:4, *NKJV*). Now her son calls to ask for prayer, and she continually reminds him of God's faithfulness in blessing his work and giving him favor. "I often pray blessing prayers for my son," she said. "But I also ask God to remove those blessings if He sees that it's the only way to turn my son's heart back to a full commitment to Him."

Recently we heard about a woman greatly concerned for her prodigal brother who was homeless and living under a bridge in a nearby city. When she asked her pastor to pray with her for her brother, he boldly prayed, "O Lord, take sleep away from him and make his pillow as a stone until he sees his need to turn back to You." A group of believers continued praying this for the man over the next several months.

At Christmas the sister bought her brother a pillow and embroidered on it "The Lord will give you rest." When she went to see him under the bridge and gave him the pillow, he looked at it and began to weep. "You have no idea what a miserable year this has been," he told her. "I haven't been able to sleep for months. Do you really think God can give me rest?" The two wept and prayed together as this prodigal returned to his heavenly Father.

Joan's strategy is to pray for every hitchhiker she passes on the road. Her own son hitchhiked across the country many times during his prodigal years, and often she had no idea where he was. She said, "When I see someone on the roadside like that, I realize it could be my son, and I always pray for that person to have an encounter with the Lord. Not long after my prodigal's hitchhiking days, he turned back to the Lord and thanked me many times for praying for his safety and salvation."

Sometimes an act of kindness goes hand in hand with prayer. We read about a young man who flunked out of school and dropped out of society, ending up homeless and alone. One bleak Thanksgiving evening, a couple found him under an overpass and gave him a box containing a wonderful turkey dinner, complete with a candle. They prayed with him and said they just wanted to let him know that God loved him. That act of kindness touched his heart and set the prodigal on the road back to God.[2]

Another mother reported she had to change her expectations and her prayer strategy when her son told her he didn't like coming home for visits because he found attending church with them offensive. "I told him that in the future I would not assume he would attend church with the family, but I would simply ask if he would care to join us. Meanwhile, we continue to pray in agreement for him. And I remind the Lord that I'm standing on Jeremiah 31:16,17—that my son 'will return from the land of the enemy.' "

Resist the Enemy

Once when I (Ruthanne) was praying for a loved one, I suddenly heard a taunting voice speak in my mind: *What makes you think praying will help? He'll never change!* For a moment I stopped praying, surprised by this interruption.

Then I realized it was the enemy. I said aloud, "Satan, I command you to be silent—you have no authority to speak to me. I resist you in Jesus' name and refuse to hear your voice. I declare that I have the mind of Christ and that my prayer is effective, according to the Word of God" (see 1 Cor. 2:16; Jas. 5:16).

One mom and her husband prayed seven times a day for their son and for the teenage boy exhibiting an ungodly influence over him: "God, we ask you to remove him from our son's life. But we ask for this friend's righteous destiny to be fulfilled—whatever plan You have for these two, we call it forth for him and for our son." Miraculously, a few weeks later that young man got a college scholarship in a distant state. Both boys eventually returned to their childhood commitment to follow Jesus.

In the days of my youngsters' wandering, I (Quin) used to walk the floor shouting, "Devil, take your hands off my children! The Bible says the seed of the righteous shall be delivered. My husband and I are righteous because Jesus shed His blood for us. Our children are our seed and they will be delivered. We have a covenant with God Almighty—that covenant stands, and you will not prevail."

Often I prayed, "Lord God, guard my children from wrong influences, wrong friends and wrong environments. Bring the right friends into their lives at the right time. Keep them from error and from being deceived." Each of my children had a dramatic return to the Lord, but I still pray this particular prayer for them.

Further Prayer Strategies

When we pray for prodigals to come home, we can expect opposition from the enemy who led them astray in the first place. We must learn to fight and engage in spiritual warfare on their behalf. The Bible offers many encouraging examples we can study for strategies, such as the story of Nehemiah rebuilding the walls of Jerusalem:

After I looked things over, I stood up and said to . . . the people, "Don't be afraid of them. Remember the Lord, who is great and awesome, and fight for your brothers, your sons and your daughters, your wives and your homes" (Neh. 4:14).

Half the people did the work of rebuilding, while the other half put on their armor and weapons to resist the enemy's attack. Nehemiah followed the strategy God gave him, and they successfully completed their task in 52 days and put fear in the hearts of their enemies.

Here are various prayer strategies we have implemented, or intercessors have shared with us, over the years:

- Ask God for specific Scripture verses on which to base your prayers for your prodigal. Praying the Word of God (sometimes singing it) for your loved ones is no doubt the strategy most widely employed by intercessors.

- Make sure you have not allowed any unforgiveness, judgment or anger toward the prodigal, or anyone else, to poison your spirit and nullify your prayers.

- Ask God to lead you into a prayer-partner relationship with another believer or support group (or form such a group yourself). Pray prayers of agreement with this confidante as the Holy Spirit leads you.

- Learn the power of binding the evil spirit(s) at work in the life of the prodigal you're praying for and loosing the person's will to no longer be captive to the devil (see Matt 16:19; 2 Tim. 2:25b,26).

· Declare the blood of Jesus over the person you are interceding for, reminding the enemy that Jesus' blood, shed for our redemption, seals the devil's certain defeat.

· Use the weapon of praise, combined with declaring Scriptures aloud, to glorify the Lord and proclaim His victory even when circumstances appear hopeless.

· Learn the value of fasting and ask the Holy Spirit to guide you in the use of this spiritual weapon (see Isa. 58:6; Matt 6:16-18).

· If you are praying for a rebellious child still living at home, pray over the child's room when he/she is not there. Anoint the door with oil, declaring aloud that the room is a place where God dwells, and command all spirits contrary to the Holy Spirit to leave. Ask the Holy Spirit to reveal truth to that child and turn him/her from darkness to light.

· Seek the Lord's guidance for creative, inoffensive ways to say "I love you" to your prodigal. Unconditional love, backed with persistent prayer, is a powerful weapon.

(See the appendix, "Waging Your Prayer Battle," for more details.)

Persistent Prayer

Sometimes we quit praying too soon. I (Quin) have a friend who told me her daughter married a man whom my friend considered nothing but a bum. So she simply quit praying for her prodigal daughter. I advised her, "Now is the time to step up your intercession for your daughter—and the son-in-law, too." She did that and saw remarkable changes in her own heart and also in her daughter's.

Our intercession is to restrict satanic forces and allow the Holy Spirit to bring conviction, repentance and godly change. It is important to be specific and persistent when waging battle in prayer. Jesus encouraged persistence in prayer by telling this parable:

> Sometimes we quit praying too soon. It is important to be specific and persistent when waging battle in prayer.

A friend comes knocking at midnight to ask his neighbor for three loaves of bread because he has an unexpected guest (see Luke 11:5-13). The neighbor is reluctant to get out of bed and give him the bread. Jesus said:

I tell you, though he will not get up and give him the bread because he is his friend, yet because of the man's [persistence] he will get up and give him as much as he needs. So I say to you: Ask and it will be given to you; seek and you will find; knock and the door will be opened to you (vv. 8,9).

Pastor Jack Hayford says of this parable:

> It is mind-boggling to understand why this passage has been used to show that prayer must earn answers through overcoming God's reluctance, as if our persistence could overcome God's resistance. In fact, Jesus is saying, "Your first barrier isn't God—it's your own hesitance to ask freely. You need to learn the kind of boldness that isn't afraid to ask—whatever the need or the circumstance."
>
> The lesson revolves around one idea: shameless boldness. . . . Boldness is your privilege. Your assignment is to ask; his commitment is to give—as much as you need.[3]

A Visible Change

Evelyn is another mom who had to look past the stark reality of her son Ken's behavior and circumstances. She'd been thrilled when he received the Lord as an eight-year-old and exuberantly shared his faith with his friends. But as the years went by and his heart grew cold toward anything to do with God, Evelyn turned to the Bible for comfort, strength and direction.

"My Bible was marked with pen and with tears as I had stood upon God's Word over and over for our family," she said. "I remember calling out Isaiah 49:25 and 54:13, reminding God that He would save our sons and daughter, that they would be taught of the Lord. And now, here was one more wayward child I would have to stand in the gap for."

For years, Evelyn had prayed Scripture prayers for her children. Now she felt she needed a new strategy—not a Scripture she already knew and could pray by rote. After Ken left home and moved back East, Evelyn went to visit him. But she was deeply grieved by his attitude, and she boarded the plane with a heavy heart for her return flight home.

"Sitting on the plane, I talked to the Lord about this son who was so obviously backslidden," she said. "I prayed, 'God, I know all the Scriptures that are there to stand on for my family, but I need something new and fresh so I can fight the good fight for my son to return to You.'

"I opened up a small book of Proverbs I had with me and began to read. Suddenly a verse seemed to leap off the page and faith was born in my heart for Ken: 'You can also be very sure that God will rescue the children of the godly' (Prov. 11:21, *TLB*). I had never noticed that Scripture, but this was a Bible version I wasn't accustomed to. I felt the Lord said, 'You may know all the Scriptures, but you don't know all the versions!' "

Little did Evelyn know that the prayer and warfare that lay ahead of her would last for 13 years. She put Ken's name in every prayer box she saw, both in this country and overseas. As her son grew increasingly hard, bitter and angry, Evelyn's heart ached to realize he was living so far below what God had for him. But she clung to God's promise—He would rescue her child.

"We learned some lessons in loving unconditionally and loving the unlovely," she said. "We learned to not preach but simply to trust our God. He kept telling us we should talk to Him more about Ken and less to Ken about Him! Ken's life was becoming deplorable, but we kept loving and praying. Eventually he began to trust us to not preach to him or condemn him, and he would turn to us when he was hurting. Once, he called and was hinting for us to pray for him. Then one day we had the courage to ask if we could pray for him, and he allowed us to. That was a real breakthrough."

Evelyn and her husband prayed that God would send people into Ken's life who would have a positive influence on him, and it happened. Ken met up with a former friend who was a Christian and eventually agreed to go to church with him. When he called home to tell his mom, she just listened, not wanting to overreact or offend him. A few days later he called again and told her he'd attended another church service. He said he felt the Lord told him this was his last chance. At that point he repented and returned to the Lord.

"Finally the day came when we were able to see our son," Evelyn shared. "I'll never forget the moment he rang the doorbell and I opened the door. There he stood, so visibly changed! Ken's countenance, dark for so many years, now was lit up with that inward glow that only Jesus can give. Yes, our prodigal son had returned! He later told us he'd been away from God since he was 10—a total of 25 years."

A Pigpen Revelation

Sarah's prayer strategy was a bit unusual. After Belinda, her adult daughter, left her husband and two children to go on the road with a long-distance truck driver, she prayed for Belinda to get a "pigpen revelation."

"It was in the pigpen that the prodigal in Jesus' parable came to his senses and decided to go home and repent," Sarah said. "My husband and I prayed that our straying daughter would recognize where she was feeding—at the pigpen—and what the Father had to offer at His table.

"We wanted her to know God's love for her, as well as ours. She'd been brought up with Christian values. We had tried to reinforce the importance of commitment and faithfulness in relationships."

Not long ago, Belinda returned home to her husband and children. Later she wrote us her own story:

I began drinking when I was very young to feel accepted and loved, and became an alcoholic. For years I sought love through relationships. The short one-night stands and a brief marriage all left me feeling cold and empty. I tried filling that emptiness with drugs, men and mostly drinking—which only made it worse.

Then I tried the "husband, two kids and a house with the white picket fence" route to happiness, but I still felt empty. So I left my husband, home and young children to follow my newest love and long-time desire to be a truck driver.

My parents and others had been praying for me for years, and especially after I hit the road trucking. Maybe it was because of those prayers that I became extremely ill and had to be hospitalized in almost every state we drove through. Finally I realized that the love I had been searching for all my life was not in a bottle or in another human relationship. The only true, lasting love is found in Jesus.

I know there is a long way to go, but the Lord has restored my marriage, and with His help there is hope for a happy ending.

"While she was gone, her husband had his own awakening," Sarah said. "He has stepped more fully into his role as the father and head of the household. Sometimes in deep crisis—such as in a pigpen—prodigals realize their need to turn back to God."

Confronting a Cultist

Another mom, after praying for months for her prodigal daughter, Heather, sensed God leading her to intervene personally in the situation. She traveled some distance to confront the young man who had bewitched Heather into following his cultish beliefs.

Challenging him face-to-face, this bold intercessor declared, "My daughter belongs to the Lord Jesus Christ, not to the god of your false religion—and she will return to Him. I'm giving you and the devil notice right now that the blinders will come off her eyes; she will see the truth and no longer be deceived. You have no right to push your antichrist religion on her."

As soon as she got back home, the mom enlisted more prayer partners to stand in the gap for Heather, binding the lying spirits that were deceiving her. The first time Heather called home after that visit, she was furious with her mom for interfering in her life.

Three months later the blinders did come off, and she called her dad to come move her back home. Even then, the young man kept pursuing her until they took measures to hide her for a season. But the once-prodigal daughter returned to the Lord and later went on several short-term missions trips, even smuggling Bibles into China.

We must remain alert and aggressive against the devil's tactics, always seeking the Lord's direction for strategy.

Intervening with Discipline

When the prodigal is a rebellious teen still living at home, parents sometimes must take drastic action in addition to their prayer strategy. A friend of ours has a son who has been committed three times to a state-run drug rehabilitation center. Each time after being released, he soon fell back into using hard drugs. Then the parents found him bleeding in their bathroom, with sliced wrists. This time they admitted him to an expensive private rehab hospital where he'll receive more personal care. And they've enlisted family and church members to pray for him until he's completely restored. He may be angry at his parents for now, but they are running interference to save his life.

Misty Bernall, mother of one of the teens who died in the Columbine High School shooting in April 1999, wrote of the disciplinary strategy she and her husband used with their rebellious daughter, Cassie. They discovered shocking evidence that Cassie and her best friend may have been planning to murder them and that she had been experimenting with drugs and the occult. They cut off Cassie's contact with her friends, enrolled her in a private Christian school and grounded her from all activities except church youth group.

For several miserable months the Bernalls endured Cassie's anger and hatred, while trying to prevent her from contacting her old friends. But when they allowed her to attend a youth retreat with a new friend she'd met at the Christian school, it proved to be the turning point they'd prayed for. Cassie came home from the retreat and announced, "Mom, I've changed."

Misty wrote, "It really seemed to be true. From then on, Cassie became a totally different person. She never talked much about that weekend and we never pressed her. But her eyes were bright, she smiled again like she hadn't for years, and she began to treat us (and her brother) with genuine respect and affection."[4]

Cassie enrolled at Columbine High School the following school year. On April 20, 1999, when two students stormed the school in a killing spree, they challenged Cassie with the question "Do you believe in God?" She said yes, and they shot her.

After her death, her parents found a book she had been reading with this sentence underlined: "All of us should live life so as to be able to face eternity at any time."[5]

Their strategy was difficult—maybe even risky. But in the end, their daughter—no longer a prodigal—was ready to meet her Lord. Despite such painful loss, they can take comfort in knowing Cassie is now with Him for all eternity.

Scripture, Vision, Declaration

When I (Quin) began diligently praying for my straying children, the Lord led me to meditate on this verse: "All your children shall be taught by the LORD, and great shall be the peace of your children" (Isa. 54:13, *NKJV*).

One of my children, who had graduated from college and was working in another state, had come home for Labor Day. After driving 50 miles to put that child on a plane after the holiday, my heart was heavy. On our way home that morning, my husband and I attended a church near the airport. During worship, I closed my eyes in prayer and suddenly had an inner vision of all three of our children with arms raised, praising God.

I said, *Lord, all three at once? Wow! That's a big order to believe for. But I will.*

Back at home, I recorded that thought in my prayer journal and continued to pray, "The Lord is my children's teacher—their peace shall be great. Thank you, Lord, that You will fulfill Your promise and they will praise You someday."

Eight months later all three asked me to meet them for Mother's Day in Orlando, where one of the children lived. We went to a church, but it was so crowded we couldn't sit together. During one of the hymns I looked about to spot them and saw all three of them with arms raised, praising God.

Before the weekend was over, I heard the stories of how God had drawn them back to Himself. My vision had become reality. But in the process I had learned an important lesson: What I declared with my mouth was important, and I needed to quote the Word of God to proclaim what He says in the matter (see Heb. 4:12).

Praise and Thanksgiving

It is important to keep our eyes on God, not on the problem, regardless of how impossible the situation appears. If we judge by outward appearances, the enemy easily intimidates us, as Goliath did with the army of Israel and tried to do to David (see 1 Sam. 17:24, 45-47).

Our human tendency is to wait until we see our prayers answered, and then offer praise. But that requires no faith.

When we offer praise to God, focusing on His mercy, love and power, it reinforces our faith and sends confusion to the enemy. By praising and thanking Him before seeing the answer, we are declaring God's victory over the evil one.

It helps to recognize that—as in the story of David and Goliath—the enemy's threats often are the most intimidating just before the victory comes. Remember David's battle cry: "It is not by sword or spear that the LORD saves; for the battle is the LORD's" (1 Sam. 17:47).

One friend heard God tell her to begin to praise and thank Him months before her son came back to God. She had labored long in her prayer closet and recognized His voice: *Begin to praise Me now, for the answer is on the way.* She did, and eventually the answer came.

Don't Give In to Discouragement

Every intercessor praying for a prodigal knows the importance of resisting discouragement when circumstances seem to get worse, not better. I (Quin) have a friend who, for years, held on to a vision God gave her of all her family occupying the same church pew on a Sunday, worshiping God together. Now only one son-in-law is missing from that vision she clings to, and a son she's prayed about for many years just came back. She bases her prayers on Proverbs 11:21 *(NASB):* "The descendants of the righteous will be delivered."

"I had to look at God's promise to me—not the circum-stances—when my son ran from the God he had loved as a youth," she said. "I just carried in my bosom this belief that God had spoken and all of my children would be back in church—which to me meant loving Him. My daughter-in-law and I prayed together for years to see a miracle in my son's life. But it happened within this past year!" She was almost shouting with joy as she spoke.

Ruth Bell Graham, who for many years prayed for her son, Franklin, to lay down his rebellion, shares this about her experience:

> Suddenly I realized the missing ingredient in my prayers had been "with thanksgiving." So I put down my Bible and spent time worshiping Him for who and what He is. This covers more territory than any one mortal can comprehend. Even contemplating what little we do know dissolves doubts, reinforces faith and restores joy.
>
> I began to thank God for giving me this one I loved so dearly in the first place. I even thanked Him for the difficult spots which taught me so much.
>
> And you know what happened? It was if someone turned on the lights in my mind and heart, and the little fears and worries that had been nibbling away in the darkness like mice and cockroaches hurriedly scuttled for cover.
>
> That was when I learned that worship and worry cannot live in the same heart: they are mutually exclusive.[6]

The Power of Negative Emotions

The enemy assaults parents of prodigals with guilt for all the things they may have done wrong in raising their children. And often they feel so crushed with shame that they distance themselves from the very people who could become prayer partners to help them with the battle. Yes, we need to admit our faults and ask our children's forgiveness for those mistakes. But getting stuck in a cycle of anger, condemnation and guilt only nullifies the effectiveness of our prayers. John White, a Christian psychiatrist with firsthand experience with a prodigal, says:

> Fear, guilt and shame are persistent enemies who may visit us in the night or greet us when we get out of bed in the morning. They must be dismissed firmly and repeatedly. They have only as much power as we are willing to lend them, and if we learn nothing else from our trials than how to conquer all three, we will certainly emerge stronger.[7]

Jean's story is one example. She wrote to us, "When my husband died, a blanket of hopelessness covered the entire family. We had been through a torturous year of watching brain cancer turn a fun-loving man into an abusive monster. We watched helplessly as a life of incredible opulence slipped out of our hands overnight. Tempers flared and tongues went untamed."

Jean's daughter sustained deep emotional wounds from her dad's verbal abuse. Hurt and angry, she wanted nothing to do with Jesus—and that included her mother and her beliefs. So to deny Jesus, she embraced the Jewish faith. The child that Jean had carried and loved and known so intimately actually went to court to "divorce" her. Humiliated, Jean didn't even attend the final court proceeding to defend herself.

"My daughter was gone, and so was her faith in Jesus," Jean wrote. "One loss on top of another. *Had all those years invested in Christian youth groups been wasted?* I wondered. Then news came

that she was studying to be a Jewish rabbi. At first I was angry—
really angry. But then one night God met me in a dream with the
assurance that all her experiences were building a foundation for
her future testimony.

"I know she has a mighty call of God on her life, and eventually she will acknowledge Jesus. The test for me has been to
accept what I cannot control. I've had to ask her forgiveness and
trust that God is bigger than her rebellion. Today we're pursuing
friendship, and I am at peace, knowing that God's Word does
not return void as I am faithful to pray it."

(See the appendix, "Waging Your Prayer Battle," for Jean's
Scripture prayer for her daughter.)

Waiting with Expectation

Of all the strategies we could suggest, waiting is perhaps the
hardest. Somehow we feel better about dealing with our prodigals if we can take action—it gives us the false illusion that we're
in control of things. The truth is, we're not in control. We have
to hand over the situation to God, remain prayerful and take
action only as He directs us.

We know the father in the parable was waiting with expectation when his errant son headed for home. Jesus said, "But while
he was still a long way off, his father saw him and was filled with
compassion for him; he ran to his son" (Luke 15:20). It's a picture of the father standing on the porch, his hand shading his
eyes from the sun, peering into the distance and thinking,
"Maybe he'll come home today."

The German theologian Helmut Thielicke argues it was not
guilt or disgust with himself that caused the prodigal to return.

He says, "It's the other way around; it was because the father and the father's house loomed up before his soul that he became disgusted with himself. . . . It was his father's influence from afar, a by-product of sudden realization of where he really belonged. . . . The consciousness of home disgusted him with the far country, actually made him realize what estrangement and lostness is."[8]

For the believer, waiting for the prodigal's return need not be a passive, "in limbo" state. The Hebrew word for "wait" comes from a root word meaning "to bind together" and figuratively means "to expect."[9] We don't wait in fear and despair. If our hope is in God, we wait expectantly for Him to intervene. And in the process, we ourselves are drawn closer to Him with bonds of love.

Prayer

Father, please give me Your wisdom to know how to pray for my prodigal. I lift his (her) specific needs to You now: (name the needs). Lord, I confess that I've felt hurt and angry at _____ because of (mention the specifics). I forgive my prodigal for hurting me and disappointing me; please help me to love him (her) with Your love and to walk in continual forgiveness. Thank You for forgiving me and enabling me to forgive those who wrong me.

Lord, I'm grateful for the power of Your Word to give comfort and guidance. Please show me appropriate Scriptures to pray for my prodigal. I release _____ into Your hands and ask You to work in his (her) life according to Your plan and purpose. I commit this person into Your care and trust You to draw him (her) to Yourself by the power of the Holy Spirit. Thank You in Jesus' name for doing a work of grace in _____'s life. Amen.

Questions to Think About

1. Have I asked God for His strategies, instead of depending on formula prayers to pray for my prodigal?
2. How can I change the overall way I relate to my prodigal as part of my strategy (offering forgiveness face-to-face or through a letter, sending a gift or expressing unconditional love in a specific way)?

Notes
1. Tom Bisset, *Why Christian Kids Leave the Faith* (n.d.; reprint, Grand Rapids, MI: Discovery House, 1992), p. 154.
2. Gregory Wenthe, "A Very Special Thanksgiving," *The Breakthrough Intercessor,* (fall 1999), pp. 28-30.
3. Jack Hayford, *Prayer Is Invading the Impossible* (New York: Ballantine Books, 1983), pp. 49-51.
4. Misty Bernall, *She Said Yes* (Farmington, PA: Plough Publishing House, 1999), p. 84.
5. Ibid., p. 107.
6. Ruth Bell Graham, *Prodigals and Those Who Love Them* (Colorado Springs: Focus on the Family, 1991), pp. 39, 40.
7. John White, *Parents in Pain* (Downers Grove, IL: InterVarsity Press, 1979), p. 159.
8. Quoted in Margie M. Lewis, *The Hurting Parent* (Grand Rapids, MI: Zondervan Publishing House, 1980), p. 138.
9. James Strong, *The New Strong's Exhaustive Concordance of the Bible,* (Nashville: Thomas Nelson, 1984), Hebrew reference #6960.

CHAPTER THREE

Putting Your Prodigal in God's Hands

I know whom I have believed, and am convinced that he is able to guard what I have entrusted to him for that day.

—2 TIMOTHY 1:12

Are we prepared to say to God, "Use anyone, anywhere, under any circumstances, to bring that lost soul to You"? Or have we prejudices (maybe hidden ones) about whom we would not want God to use?[1]

—JOY DAWSON

Ll parents who pray for their children eventually recognize the necessity of releasing them into God's
hands. Sounds like a simple matter, but if you've
been in that place, you know how difficult it can be. I (Ruthanne)
struggled with this one day years ago when I was praying Isaiah
54:13 for my son, paraphrasing the verse like this: "My son shall
be taught of the Lord, and great shall be his peace."

Suddenly I was aware of God's still, small voice speaking to
my heart: *If you want Me to be his teacher, then you must get out of the
way.*

I responded by explaining to God that this headstrong 17-
year-old was on a collision course with a brick wall. Because of a
bad report from his teacher, I had set an appointment for my
son to meet with a tutor who would coach him for his final algebra exam. Claiming the problems were his teacher's fault, my
son angrily declared that he wouldn't go to a tutor.

Maybe hitting a brick wall is the only way he will learn, the Holy
Spirit whispered. *After all, how did you learn your lessons?*

It's true for most of us that we learn best by hard experience.
I agonized over the consequences my son would face later if he
failed algebra, but I obeyed the Lord and canceled the appointment. I discovered how painful it is to truly commit your child
into God's hands.

Sure enough, my son failed his final algebra exam. He did
pass the course, but with the lowest grade he had ever made in
any class, and he lost his membership in the National Honor
Society. Almost a year went by before the full consequences
became apparent.

He had applied to a top university for admission and a
scholarship. After passing several levels of the acceptance
process, he was in the pool of candidates for the few slots open
in the school of architecture. But he didn't make the final cut.

I was sure it was because of his low grade in 11th-grade algebra.

The day he came home and found his rejection letter he stormed upstairs in a fit of anger and disappointment. "Oh, Lord," I prayed, "I know he had to learn this lesson, but it's so painful to see him devastated like this."

The Lord spoke very gently in the midst of my tears. *Don't worry, I won't hurt him any more than I have to—he was Mine before he was yours, and I love him more than you do.* God was gracious to open another opportunity for my son to study architecture and has faithfully continued to be his teacher. But for me, that experience was the beginning of a "letting go" process that has continued through the years.

Forgiveness Brings Healing

Whether the prodigal you're praying for is a child, a sibling, a parent, a spouse—whoever it might be—eventually you must put him or her in God's hands and trust Him to do a work of grace in that person's life. A mother wrote to share her experience of doing just that:

At age 14, Dawn began showing signs of hostility toward my husband, her stepfather. Up until this time she had called him Daddy and insisted on having her last name changed to his. But when she rebelled, she contacted the authorities at her school and told them she was going to run away if we didn't allow her to live with her girlfriend and her family.

The court got involved and I lost custody of her. She became a ward of the court, then was placed in a succession of foster homes. When we would see her in court she would swear at us and make obscene gestures. It broke my heart to see her like this.

Because of her extreme hostility, the Child Protective Services suspected she'd been molested, and they thought my husband may have been the one who did it. Later, we learned it was a friend's 41-year-old father, who wanted to marry her.

The eight months that Dawn was out of our home were nearly unbearable for me. I became desperate before God. On Mother's Day Sunday in church, our pastor spoke of the woman with the issue of blood and how she touched the hem of Jesus' garment and was healed. That morning, in prayer, I pressed in and touched the hem of His garment—somehow I knew God had heard my cry. Don't ask me how, I just knew! I placed my daughter completely in God's hands and trusted Him to bring about a miracle.

Shortly after that experience, God began turning the situation around through some amazing events. My husband chose to forgive Dawn for her rebellion, and our relationship with her was healed. Then the court returned custody to us. Considering all the circumstances, it had seemed impossible that our prodigal would ever return home. But God is faithful, and He restored our family.

Today Dawn is my best friend. When she was 24, my husband even got to adopt her. Only God could have put these broken pieces together again.

Receiving One's Prodigal

Suppose your prodigal asks to come home and shows regret and remorse but no repentance. Or say he's still strung out on drugs.

Or alcohol. Each family must make that difficult decision, with God's direction. No hard and fast principle applies to receiving home one's prodigal.

If he will have an adverse effect on younger children still at home, some parents consider it a valid reason to say no. Yet others receive a child who is addicted in order to nurse him or her back to health. Or, as Jane and her husband did for their son Jeff, they receive a child to pray for him at close range.

Jane fasted, interceded and travailed in prayer for hours on behalf of Jeff when he was addicted to drugs and alcohol. Even when he was stoned and roaring off on his motorcycle, she continually prayed this prayer of relinquishment: "God, I free You to do anything You have to do to make Jeff a man of God. Lord, come and establish Your throne in his life." She and her husband also prayed over the objects in his room.

Many months later, when he overdosed on drugs, Jeff sought help. A Christian befriended him, pointed him toward Jesus and was instrumental in Jane's prayers being answered. Today Jeff has an ongoing relationship with the Lord.

The Enemy's Power Broken

Beth wrote to tell us of her heartbreak when she learned that her daughter had gotten involved in lesbianism. Beth and her husband hadn't taken seriously Lynn's lack of interest in dolls and dancing lessons or her preference for boys' clothes and aggressive athletics. There had been signs of rebellion from time to time, but it was at a Christian camp for training youth leaders that Lynn began her first same-sex relationship at age 18.

"The anguish and guilt we experienced turned to anger and accusations as the years went by," Beth wrote. "Year after year, disappointment followed disappointment. As siblings married, Christmases and family gatherings became nightmares as the other four children tried to learn to handle the embarrassment of Lynn's lifestyle. Weddings, gift-giving, and all holidays were painful. And the problem was intensified by Lynn's addiction to alcohol and nicotine."

More than 20 years passed, with many prayers and much fasting. They saw no outward evidence of change in Lynn as they continued to trust God in the situation. Then two of Beth's friends and prayer partners visited her when they were in town to speak for a conference. They prayed and did spiritual warfare specifically for Lynn, and sensed a spiritual breakthrough.

"After they left, I went to take a shower and had an overwhelming awareness that the enemy's power had been broken over Lynn," Beth said. "Later I learned these two intercessors had continued to pray for our daughter as they traveled that day, but I definitely felt the work was done. Now, 22 years after Satan drew Lynn into his net, the God to whom we dedicated her at birth has brought her to Himself again.

"Once when I was praying that Christ would be formed in her, God gave me a vision of Lynn as a marquis-cut diamond. Now I know He is fashioning her for His glory. Her whole appearance and demeanor have changed. She is talking about the Lord, quoting Scriptures, and loving people and members of our family like never before. She's the sweet child she used to be as a little girl."

Of course the many prayers Beth and her husband and others had prayed for Lynn all those years were important. We have the promise of James 5:16: "Pray for each other so that you may be healed. The prayer of a righteous man [or woman] is powerful and effective."

But when a critical moment arrives in the life of a prodigal, God often issues a specific call to prayer, such as when he spoke to Ananias to go and pray for Saul (see Acts 9:10-19). Just as Ananias did, Beth's two prayer-warrior friends obeyed the assignment God called them to. And it proved to be a turning point in the prayer battle for Lynn.

Pastor Ron Mehl writes:

When God calls you to pray for your child—or any child of God—it is no casual, random thing. This might be the hour in which that person is dealing with an all-important issue or staggering under some crushing load. Someone "watching over their souls" may be God's special provision to help and deliver them in that moment.[2]

He Heard Me—His Mom—Praying

Sometimes a child goes astray for reasons we may never understand, even when we've tried our best to be a godly parent. Sue's story is an example of this. She wrote that her son James, a big blond, blue-eyed guy, always wanted to be number one or the very best he could be. He was a top student in his class and never gave any serious problems until his junior and senior years in high school. But then things changed for the worse. Here is her story:

First, James began experimenting with alcohol, then drugs—I believe he just wanted to be one of the "in" group. His best friends were kids of respected people in the community, but they were drinking and smoking pot. One rule we enforced in our home was that regardless of what time the children came home, they were to come in and give Mom a good-night kiss. James was always prompt. I could always tell what kind of shape he was in by his good-night kiss. If he stayed in the bathroom a long time brushing his teeth and gargling before he came to kiss me, I knew he had been up to something—and I could smell it.

Sometimes a child goes astray for reasons we may never understand, even when we've tried our best to be a godly parent.

After starting his freshman year at college, early one November morning the Lord woke me up saying, *Your son's life is in danger.* When I questioned the Lord, I heard Him say again, *Your son's life is in danger.* My husband was on duty at the hospital that night, so I called three of my prayer partners and we all prayed for James.

At 7:00 A.M. I called his dorm room. His roommate actually tried to cover up for him—said he was at the library. I knew that was a lie. I kept calling until finally the roommate told me James and some of his friends had gone to a particular well-known campsite. Then I really started praying. I knew the place was a favorite party spot, and that James was in trouble. It was below freezing and snowing, and he had no type of camping gear that I knew of.

I went down to my laundry room—my prayer closet—and pled with the Lord to save James, then I released him completely into God's hands. Whether I got to see him alive again on this earth or not, the important thing was for James to receive forgiveness for his sins and an assurance of salvation. After praying for a while, peace entered my heart. I knew my son was in the *best* care.

When my husband got home later that morning I shared what had happened. About three in the afternoon James called. I told him how I'd been praying so fervently for him, and he admitted that he and his friends were doing a lot of things—alcohol, LSD and pot. At one point early that morning, James had found himself all alone, poking a stick in the campfire. Completely mesmerized by the flames, he began thinking of hell as he stared at the fire. Then he said it was as if he heard me—his mom—praying.

After our conversation I drove almost three hours to pick him up at the campus and bring him back home. That night when my husband and I laid hands on James and prayed over him, I knew in my heart his life would be different. After church on Sunday I drove him back to school. It was as if he had walked back into a den of wolves where drugs and alcohol were so accessible. But through continual prayer by me and my husband and our prayer-warrior friends, we determined Satan was not going to have our son.

At spring break, James attended a missions conference where God softened his heart. When he went back to school, Satan threw every temptation he could at him—drugs, alcohol, sex. But James had felt the presence of God and he was not going to let Him go. After his freshman year I moved him out of the dorm. This was probably the sickest day of my life—seeing how he had lived for 10 months. I can't even describe the evil that was present in that dorm.

He moved into an old farmhouse with some decent guys—actually one was our daughter's future husband—and got involved in a college outreach organization. He was still drawn to the party people at college for a while, but during this period he began to understand the difference between darkness and light (see Eph. 5:8-21).

By the time the next spring break rolled around, James went back to the missions conference. Finally he came to the end of himself and fully repented before the Lord. He not only experienced the presence of God, but dedicated himself for His service. Now he is enrolled in the physical therapy training program at college and married to a godly young woman. Their desire is to serve the Lord all their lives.

We fought this prayer battle for several years before we saw results. My advice to mothers, fathers and prayer warriors: Stay on your knees—your prodigals will come home.

An Encourager
When I Needed One

Once when I (Quin) was downhearted because I had not seen any positive change in my own children, God sent Paul Billheimer and his wife, Jenny, to have a meal at our table and to encourage me. He admonished me to never stop believing the promises God had already given me for them. Then he shared about his own mother's "power prayers," as he called them, which he wrote about in his classic book *Destined for the Throne*. I read and reread this passage many times:

My mother used these weapons [mentioned in 2 Cor. 10:3-5] on me. I was as hostile to God as any sinner. I was fighting with all my might. But the time came when it was easier to lay down my arms of rebellion than to continue my resistance. The pressure exerted upon me by the Holy Spirit became so powerful that I voluntarily sought relief by yielding my rebellious will. The wooing of divine love was so strong that of my own free will I fell into the arms of redeeming grace. I became a willing "captive."[3]

Mr. Billheimer says the use of spiritual weapons does not violate the free will of the rebels, but "changes them from rebellion to voluntary cooperation."[4]

The Finger of God

Another mom and her former prodigal share from different perspectives the story of his return. Twins Ted and Dave were born into a Christian family—generations of believers who trusted God and heard His voice. Their mother, Carla, never doubted these two would continue that legacy. After high school graduation, Dave entered a Christian university and Ted signed up for a five-year tour of duty with the Navy.

Though Ted tried to stay close to the Lord, a feeling of deep emptiness and loneliness overcame him, and he yearned to be popular. Soon he was entangled in relationships with women that crushed him emotionally. Drinking and partying at nightclubs with a fast crowd escalated to experimenting with drugs.

"I had no clue as to what was going on, but I felt an urgency to pray especially hard for Ted," Carla said. "One day a sense of deep loss hit me—as if Ted had died—and I began mourning in the spirit. Then Dave called and said he'd dreamed that his twin brother had drowned—which was a possibility because he was a rescue swimmer.

"We began to call the many prayer warriors in our family to pray for Ted. We felt we were fighting for his life, both physically and spiritually. After a time we experienced a breakthrough as a deep peace settled into our spirits."

Ted had gotten deep into drugs and the Rave scene, trying to make it to every party. But during his last year in the Navy, two significant events happened: one divine, the other evil. He wrote about it:

Over Christmas my parents talked to me about my focus for the future and then they prayed for me, putting me in God's hands. I felt like the finger of God was on my forehead and I couldn't deny that He was touching me. I even told my friends I was touched by God, and they believed me. But I still enjoyed my old lifestyle too much to leave.

One night after having two hits of acid, suddenly I felt I was staring at Satan. He said, "It is over!" Looking at him, I said, "What?" He repeated, "It's over. Game's over." I replied, "No, it's not." He said, "You lose."

I stopped partying for two months, except for one Rave where I danced all night long but didn't do drugs. I knew I was leaving the Navy to go home and find God. My last day on duty, no one was around to say good-bye, so I quietly climbed into my car and headed for home. I felt my old life literally falling away.

I didn't talk a lot the next two months except to my family. I felt like a child and saw the world as a place that I must hide from until I had grown. When I talked about my time in the Navy I wanted to cry, because I saw how the darkness had surrounded me and how my heavenly Father had spared me. God told me He never let me fall too far, and when I look back I see that. I had to be lost so that I could understand what it is like to be found.

Lost. Found. Now two years later, this prodigal has been providing a place for street kids to hang out on Saturday nights and he is engaged to a wonderful Christian woman. Ted and Dave work with other on-fire young people to put on Christian "Raves" at all-night fests that are packed with intercessors doing spiritual warfare.

Still Waiting

It's encouraging to receive such reports of answered prayer, but many parents still are waiting for a spiritual breakthrough and for relationships to be restored.

One mother wrote of the disappointment she and her husband have experienced since their adult son, married for 17 years, divorced his wife and married someone he had met through the Internet. They have yet to meet his new wife. And their former daughter-in-law and the three children have moved to another state, so they seldom get to see their grandchildren.

"Our son comes to town on business fairly often and stays with us," she said, "but we hardly see him. He hasn't completely turned his back on God, but our contact with him is on a very superficial level. We just keep praying for him and putting the situation in God's hands. We feel the Lord has impressed us that it will take five years before the brokenness is totally healed."

Even in the midst of her painful situation, this mom finds hope in the word God has given them. When we're obedient in committing our prodigals to the Lord, He is faithful to give us a prophetic word or a Scripture to sustain us as we wait for a breakthrough.

Suppose you are still wallowing in disappointment or guilt. Perhaps you are bitter and antagonistic toward the prodigal who has turned his back on your faith. What then? One mother and author has a suggestion:

> Sometimes I tell people to take all this hurt into their hands, hold their hands up to God and give it all to Him. He's the only one who can give peace. He's the only one who can bring our children through to their God-given potential. They may not be meeting our expectations and dreams, but God can fulfill His will in their lives if we let Him. As parents, it is important for us to allow Him to guide our children and work in them without blocking Him with our anger, bitterness and sorrow.[5]

Author Catherine Marshall once shared an entry from her journal about the Lord speaking to her about her family. She wasn't dealing with a prodigal situation at the time, but her words are pertinent to our topic:

> I was shown that my husband, my children, and my grandchildren are not mine, but God's. He's not only as concerned as I am for them, but loves them far more than I ever could. Therefore, I was to take my possessive, self-centered hands off—strictly off. So, in an act of relinquishment, I did this.
>
> Then came a beautiful touch. I was reading in the Psalms when suddenly these words leapt from the page:

"The Lord will perfect that which concerns me . . ." (Ps. 138:8, *NKJV*).

I could—and did—claim this promise promptly for my family. Years ago the Lord began a work in these lives. It's His business to perfect what He started. He has promised that He will. I've claimed and accepted that promise. It's as good as done. My heart is steadily rejoicing. Weights and weights have been lifted from me.[6]

Catherine went on to share the prayer of relinquishment she prayed—an excellent example for us to follow as we put our loved ones in God's hands:

I confess, Lord, my demanding spirit. I've told You how the prayer could be answered. To my shame, I've even bargained with You. No wonder my spirit is so sore and weary.

Now, Lord, I want to give up all this self-effort. I want You in my life more than I want this thing I've been praying for to happen. So by an act of my will, I relinquish all this to You, removing myself so You can be free to do Your will in me, or through me, or around me.

How grateful I am to realize that the answer to my prayer may not depend upon me at all![7]

Prayer

Lord, help me to relinquish my loved one completely into Your hands. So often I grab him (her) back and worry and fret even when I pray. I rehearse in my mind—and to You—all the sordid details of how bad this situation is. Forgive me for forgetting that I must surrender every aspect of_____'s life to You. I know I can trust You to bring back this prodigal in Your way and in Your time—and through whatever circumstances You see fit. Help me let go and give_____ to You unreservedly. I ask in Jesus' Name. Amen.

Questions to Think About

1. Am I willing to give God permission to do whatever it takes to draw my prodigal to Himself?
2. What steps can I take to stop trying to control circumstances in this person's life?

Notes
1. Joy Dawson, *Intercession: Thrilling and Fulfilling* (Seattle: YWAM Publishing, 1997), p. 41.
2. Ron Mehl, *God Works the Night Shift* (Sisters, OR: Multnomah Publishers, 1994), p. 144.
3. Paul Billheimer, *Destined for the Throne* (Fort Washington, PA: Christian Literature Crusade, 1975), pp. 67, 68.
4. Ibid.
5. Joyce Thompson, *Preserving a Righteous Seed* (Dallas: CTM Publishing, 1998), p. 37.
6. Catherine Marshall, *Teachings from Catherine Marshall's Journals* (Lincoln, VA: Breakthrough, Inc., n.d.), p. 29.
7. Ibid., p. 31.

CHAPTER FOUR

Prodigals in Prison

He has sent me to proclaim freedom for the prisoners and recovery of sight for the blind, to release the oppressed.

—LUKE 4:18

I prayed repeatedly, "Father, do anything to Richard to bring him back except put him in jail."

One day, when I let Him, God said to me,
Why don't you want him in jail?

I gave what I thought was the obvious answer.
"Father, it would ruin his life!"

To my surprise God asked again,

Why don't you want him in jail? . . .
I examined my response and said, "Well, to tell You the truth, if
Richard ended up in jail his name would be in the papers.
We live in a small town and people in the world love to
publish anything bad about ministers and the Church.
Then what would they think about us?"

God answered kindly, You see, your problem is one of pride.
And I realized that I was less concerned about how jail would
affect Richard's life than I was fearful of having my
name dragged through the dust.[1]

—PASTOR PETER LORD

For many parents of prodigals who end up in prison, it must seem that the very worst has happened. But even in the darkness and bondage of a prison cell, the Holy Spirit is able to minister light and freedom. Corrie ten Boom once said in one of her talks, "When the worst happens, the best is yet to be."

A mother whose daughter was arrested and jailed on drug charges went through what she called her greatest nightmare. At the hearing she saw her child escorted into the courtroom in handcuffs and shackles; then she visited her in jail.

She said, "Inside, I was screaming, *I cannot go through this.* But the Lord walked me through when my legs were weak and my emotions stretched to the limit."

At last report the daughter had completed two phases of rehab, was employed and doing well. She has told her mother many times that God was hounding her while she was away from Him—watching out for her, keeping her alive and sending people and situations into her life to give her a chance to respond.

"I've never met a recovered addict or alcoholic yet who does not attest to the fact that they knew someone was praying for them, or they wouldn't be alive," the mother wrote.[2]

When a police sergeant phoned Peter and Johnnie Lord at 5:00 A.M. one morning, saying their son had been jailed for drug possession, they had to make a decision. Pastor Lord wrote:

> I had told Richard that if he got arrested for his drug use we were not going to bail him out. "Make sure you are prepared to live with the consequences of your choices," I had said. . . . God had to strengthen our backbones to enable us to leave Richard in that jail—and He did. It was probably one of the best, and toughest, learning experiences Richard had. It certainly made a memorable impression on us.[3]

Richard not only returned to the Lord, he later studied for the ministry and became a pastor.

Finding Freedom Behind Bars

Recently, my friend Anne's son (we'll call him Joe) wrote from prison to let me (Quin) know he is now serving God. Here's a portion of his letter:

Christian family members played an important role in my formative years. Outside of what I learned in my own home, other relatives were highly involved. For instance, my maternal grandmother taught Sunday School to kids in our church and my paternal grandfather was a deacon. I definitely grew up being influenced by Christian family members. Unfortunately, my life did not turn out quite like you would have expected from one who grew up in such an environment.

Despite making a decision to become a Christian and be baptized at an early age, I turned my back on God and began having brushes with the law before I was 13. Eventually I ended up spending roughly four of my teen years making the rounds of various boys' ranches, juvenile homes, reform schools and jails.

Since then I've spent more than 25 years of my adult life in prison, with a slim likelihood of me ever getting out. But those earlier years with my family were not a total washout. The time came when I found myself at a crossroads, with God putting it to me real simply: "Choose." Had I not grown up in a Christian environment and been supported through those wasted years by the vigilant prayers of my family and other Christians, I might not have been open to God or even comprehended what He was telling me. Fortunately for me, I was open and did comprehend His message.

Now, I find God is teaching me how to find His freedom even behind bars, regardless of how hopeless my situation appears. This was possible only when I chose to submit to God's will, and I thank Him greatly for all the wonderful family and other Christians He used over the years to prepare me for making this decision.

What a thrill to receive his letter! I remember the day more than 20 years ago when I first prayed with Anne, Joe's mom, who is one of my prayer partners. She told me then of the process she'd been through to get her own heart right with God before she could pray effectively for her son in prison.

"After becoming a Christian, I was reading my Bible and praying for Joe one day," she said. "When I got to the second chapter of Joel, this verse pierced my heart: ' "Even now," declares the

LORD, "return to me with all your heart, with fasting and weeping and mourning" ' (v. 12). Through that verse, God shone a spotlight on my heart, revealing my bitterness, anger and unforgiveness. I repented—with fasting, weeping and prayer. And I asked God to change me. Then I began to claim the promise of Joel 2:25: 'I will repay you for the years the locusts have eaten.'

"Even though I hadn't been the kind of parent my son needed in his growing-up years, I believed that God would restore the years the evil 'locusts' had eaten from my life and that Joe would accept the Lord."

For Anne, it was a big leap of faith. What did it mean that God would restore? Get her son out of prison? Bring him to the knowledge of his need for a Savior? Protect him from bullies in prison? She knew she would not limit God. Most of all, she wanted to see her son become a follower of Jesus. Though it took years of prayer and believing in God's words to her, Anne saw the greatest of all miracles. Joe did accept Jesus as his Lord, even in prison.

Today Anne is one of the most joyous Christian mothers I've ever known. What's more, she's a strong intercessor for her state's prison system—praying for wardens, inmates, guards and chaplains. Many mothers might be so devastated at having a son in prison that they would never think to intercede for others there. But Anne is ever grateful to the Good Shepherd for finding her lost lamb behind bars.

Putting Up Bail

Lou, another praying mother, shares her story of seeing a prodigal son go to jail. While still in high school, a wanderlust seemed to drive Daren to want to see the country. Lou and her husband promised that if he would finish school, then attend his sister's wedding, they would help him and send him with their blessing. He agreed, though not very willingly.

Then he began traveling, mostly by hitchhiking. He said that almost every time someone picked him up it turned out to be a Christian who advised him, "Go home." Once he stole money for drugs, using his dad's hunting knife to threaten his victim— though he never intended to cause bodily harm.

A year went by as his parents faithfully prayed for their son to return to the Lord and to his home. The wanderlust continued until Daren finally came to the end of himself.

One night, as Lou was reading her Bible about one o'clock in the morning, she heard a knock at the door. When she opened the door, Daren fell into her arms and said, "Well, I'm ready to give myself up."

When he confessed his part in an attempted armed robbery, he could have faced six years in jail. Parents and friends not only prayed, they wrote letters to the judicial system, appealing for leniency. Daren was convicted, but after three weeks in jail he was released on a large bail, which his parents provided by mortgaging their home.

"After his jail experience, he came home a changed young man," Lou reported. "He stopped running with the wrong crowd and doing drugs. Instead he stayed home, got a job and started attending church with us."

Daren never took another step of disobedience that would have landed him back in jail or caused his parents to lose their home. Now, 25 years later, he is married, with two sons. He's a delightful Christian man. His parents continue to thank God for bringing back their prodigal. Lou, who ministers to women in prison, shares her son's story to help reach other prodigals and to encourage those who are praying for them.

"Charge It to Me"

Let's look at the story of one of the fugitives in the Bible—Onesimus. He was a runaway slave from the household of Philemon, a wealthy friend of the apostle Paul. The church at Colosse met in his home.

Although we don't know exactly why Onesimus ran away, we do know that when he got to Rome he crossed paths with the apostle Paul, a prisoner under house arrest. It could be that Onesimus had been arrested and assigned to servant duties in the house where Paul was being held. At any rate, Paul wasted no time in leading Onesimus to Christ and discipling him.

It's clear that Paul wanted to keep Onesimus as a coworker, but first he sought to bring reconciliation between the slave and the master he had wronged. So he sent the runaway back to Philemon with a letter of recommendation.

Although the church in Colosse met in Philemon's house, he had not converted this particular slave to the Christian faith. The Early Church did not preach against slavery directly, but its leaders referred to master and slave as being equal before God (see Gal. 3:28), and both were accountable for their behavior (see Eph. 6:5-9). To run away meant severe punishment, even death, should the slave be caught. So Onesimus was taking a big chance in returning to his owner.

Paul's letter to Philemon included a blank check, so to speak. He said, "If he has done you any wrong or owes you anything, charge it to me. . . . I will pay it back—not to mention that you owe me your very self" (vv. 18,19). Of course, Paul was the one who had led Philemon to Christ, so the slave owner owed the apostle a debt of gratitude.

Jesus, by His sacrificial death on a cross, purchased freedom from eternal death for every person who will accept that pardon. His act says to Father God, "See that one—charge his debt to me. He's one of mine."

I (Quin) have a friend for whom this story became a way out of her self-made prison of bitterness. Her prodigal son, whom she had adopted when he was just a few years old, had hurt her deeply and she struggled with unforgiveness. Though he was grown and had left home, he was still rebellious, belligerent and foulmouthed whenever he was around her. He showed her only contempt.

One day she asked God for help in overcoming her resentful, judgmental attitudes toward this son and his treatment of her. She felt the Lord led her to read the small book of Philemon. When she closed the Bible it was as though Jesus boomed out of heaven at her, "Marcy, if he owes you anything, charge it to Me. But don't forget you owe Me your very life. I love your son as much as I love you."

With tears of repentance, she forgave her son. Then she made a decision to walk out that forgiveness. Whenever he came to her home after that and continued slamming doors and yelling at her, she'd silently breathe, "Jesus, I charge it to You." She has been able to keep her cool whenever he explodes, reminding herself that she's not responsible for his behavior—only her own. And she's no longer chained in a prison of bitterness.

Now she prays for him with new awareness of his need for the Savior and a greater appreciation of what Jesus has done for her. As Marcy discovered, this approach clears the air, enabling the restoration of a loving relationship, and lays a biblical foundation for us to receive God's forgiveness (see Matt. 6:14,15).

Forgiveness is available for every problem. God doesn't want us to save up for the "biggies." Sometimes parents dismiss their child's hurt feelings or ignore what seems trivial, not realizing that even small things can develop into serious relational roadblocks. In some cases we can help prevent our children from becoming prodigals by dealing with small problems when they arise, asking for forgiveness when necessary and remaining faithful in prayer.

Grandmothers—Important Prayer Pillars

Stephen is a young man who seemed destined for destruction because of his life of drug addiction and crime. For 28 years, Joan, his paternal grandmother, faithfully prayed for him. As soon as he was born, Joan felt the Lord showed her He had chosen this child's name and someday he would be like Stephen in the Bible (see Acts 6:5,8). As he grew up, Joan often told him that God had a plan for his life.

After Stephen's parents divorced, an alcoholic, drug-addicted mother and stepfather raised him. He began using drugs by age 13, and at 19 served his first jail term on a drug possession charge. In and out of jail for the next several years, finally he was sentenced to three-and-a-half years for a firearm felony. During this jail term he committed his life to the Lord. But when he got out after serving less than a third of the sentence, he reverted to his old ways.

"I thought I was a Christian now," he said. "But I immediately got involved in an adulterous relationship; then I got a job by lying on the application form, and before long I was doing drugs again. When I got fired for lying, I began manufacturing methamphetamines and dealing drugs full-time."

When Stephen got word that his mother had overdosed on drugs and been rushed to the hospital, he at last became desperate. He begged God to heal his mother and promised he would stop doing and dealing drugs. God mercifully saved his mother's life, but Stephen couldn't keep his end of the bargain. Soon he was doing drugs again . . . and was arrested again.

"That night I told God I would do the time if only He would come into my heart again," he said. "I spent the whole night praying. Jesus had gotten my attention now, and I could no longer run. I had been denying Him for four years. Not only did He come back into my heart, but He gave me peace that I had never known before. I knew I wasn't playing games with God anymore."

No intercessor wants the prodigal she's praying for to go to jail, but in some cases that's exactly where the wanderer will have an encounter with God.

Stephen was sentenced to two years in prison, but at last he truly had surrendered his heart to God. While serving his time, he was able to witness and minister to other prisoners. Joan was able to supply him with Bibles, books, tapes and videos, and he loved studying the Word.

"When Stephen was released from prison," Joan said, "he came to live with my husband and me. God has brought the joy of the Lord to our home and revival through Stephen. When we visited him in prison, one guard told me how the atmosphere changed when Stephen arrived and shared God's love. He was baptized, and the chaplain sent us a video so we could witness this special event. Stephen hopes to attend Bible school and study music so he can lead others in worshiping God."

No intercessor wants the prodigal she's praying for to go to jail, but in some cases that's exactly where the wanderer will have an encounter with God. We thank God for those Christians who work among delinquents and prisoners—who see beyond the bars, sense their potential and care for their souls. Fawn Parish is one of these. She wrote:

> I once taught incarcerated teenagers. Many of my students had committed murder and other serious crimes. . . . I had high expectations of what they could learn. I would bring them good literature that explored what it meant to be human. I would ask them to search the inner lands of their minds and hearts. I was aware that God could turn any one of them on a dime, capture their hearts and transform them. I knew that God had expectations for them that transcended their present reality.[4]

"I'll Never Run Away Again"

One mom wrote us of the grief one son put her through. Thinking back, she remembered when this son's personality changed radically. After he'd endured antirabies shots, he no longer was their sweet, gentle little boy. He often became angry, sullen, offensive, belligerent and sassy, then he'd be sweet again. Later she read in a magazine that the antirabies shot sometimes affects parts of the brain and changes one's personality. *Oh, Lord, what did we do to our child?* she inwardly cried.

Rob gave his heart to the Lord at 17, but within a few years was running from Him. Both his dad and his brother died in a tragic accident. Then his marriage fell apart and he owed more child support than he could pay. He stole a car, got arrested, jumped bail and became a fugitive from justice. All the while his mom was standing in the prayer gap for him.

"I sang a special song during that time entitled, 'Rejoice, Rejoice, My Son Is Coming Home Again,' " she told us. "I cried, then laughed as I could see Rob coming home to Jesus. The words fit my prayers, for they were from the parable of the prodigal son in Scripture."

Sometime later he finally was apprehended and put in a correctional facility. From there he wrote this letter:

There is just so much that looks hopeless right now. However, I know God is going to help me through all of it. You see, I gave my life back to Him the other day, and now, I feel more peace than I have had in 20 years. I didn't do it as a bargain to try and get out of this mess. Actually, God has been convicting me for more than 20 years, and I have just been running away . . . but He caught me. I know in my heart now that I will never run from Him again. . . . I may not do everything exactly as I should for the rest of my life, but I will live it with Him in it.

Rob admitted that during his 20 years away from God, hardly a Sunday morning rolled around that he didn't feel he should watch a Christian program on television. But he didn't. All those years his faithful, praying mom never gave up hope on her prodigal. She wrote, "I do rejoice. Because of God's mercy, my prodigal has come home to Jesus."

Double Blessing

It's wonderful to see the overflow or domino effect that some-times happens when we pray for family members. Lorraine is an example of this principle. For years she prayed for her brother Stuart and his family to come to Christ. His typical response was, "Don't bother me with talk about religion." As hard as she prayed for him, she saw no positive results.

Then one day Lorraine's brother called to tell her his son, Bart, who had been in jail for theft, was getting out soon. He'd been incarcerated for selling stolen items, which he was doing to support his drug habit, and his marriage had broken up. "Can you and your husband help him find a place to stay?" Stuart asked. "The jail is not that far from where you live."

Lorraine and her husband agreed to invite Bart to stay with them. Later they learned he had had an encounter with God while in jail. A chaplain had asked him, "Would you allow me to pray for you?" Bart agreed, and as the chaplain prayed, Bart felt an energy like fire shoot through him as the power of God touched him. After that he never missed a chapel or Bible study at the jail.

Lorraine's nephew came to live in her upstairs bedroom. As a spiritually hungry and thirsty new Christian, he began to work in her husband's Christian ministry, attended church regularly and eventually married a wonderful woman he had met through a support group for former drug addicts.

At first Bart was reluctant to let his dad, Stuart, know that he was now a committed Christian. Though he'd gone to church youth camp while a teenager and occasionally attended church, he had not been a true believer. But as he grew in faith after his jail experience, Bart became eager for his father to know Christ in an intimate way.

Lorraine knew that God was answering her prayers for her brother when Stuart agreed to attend a Christian men's rally with her husband and Bart. In the meeting the leader encouraged the men to get acquainted with those sitting around them in the stadium bleachers. "Tell the man sitting behind you how you came to know the Lord," the speaker said.

Bart had slipped out of his seat for a minute, but a man turned to shake Stuart's hand and asked how he'd come to the Lord. All Stuart could say to him was, "I was baptized as a baby and I married an Episcopalian."

A few moments later, when Bart returned, Stuart said, "Son, I didn't have an answer for that man as to how I came to know the Lord."

"Well, Dad, would you like to accept Him right now?" Bart asked.

"Yes, I would."

As Bart led his own father in a salvation prayer, Lorraine's prayers of more than 40 years were answered at last. After the meeting they gathered in her kitchen and Stuart wept as he told her how he had received Christ.

"Is Dad looking down from heaven and witnessing this?" he asked.

"Yes," Lorraine said, "I believe he is."

Now Stuart reads the Bible every day and prays for other family members who have not yet committed their lives to Christ. In the meantime, Bart has become a department manager in the company owned by his uncle, and he and his wife are teaching their children to walk in God's ways.

The lesson from Lorraine's experience? Never give up praying, believing and standing on the promises of God for your family members. You never know what unusual circumstances the Lord will use—even a jail experience—to answer those prayers and bring reconciliation and healing to your family.

If you are a parent of a child in trouble with the law, you may think your nightmare will never end. But not only is God watching over your child, He's in the dark valley with you. You can draw strength and comfort from His love.

Prayer

Lord, I'm so grateful You didn't give up on me. That knowledge gives me hope that You won't give up on my prodigal either, even in prison. Bring the people of Your choice to help him (her) lead a life for You. Keep _____(name) from discouragement and depression. Give him (her) peace despite circumstances. Protect _____ from the bullies who would try to bring physical harm, and give him (her) favor with authorities and friendships with other Christians. I thank You, Lord. Amen.

Questions to Think About

1. Do I truly believe "When the worst happens, the best is yet to be"?
2. What positive results already have come from this prison experience?
3. What good results might come in the future?

Notes

1. Peter Lord, *Keeping the Doors Open* (Tarrytown, NY: Fleming H. Revell, 1992), pp. 53, 54.
2. From *A Woman's Guide to Getting Through Tough Times,* © 1998 by Quin Sherrer and Ruthanne Garlock. Published by Servant Publications, Box 8617, Ann Arbor, Michigan, 48107, p. 56. Used with permission.
3. Peter Lord, *Keeping the Doors Open,* pp. 17, 61, 62.
4. Fawn Parish, *Honor: What Love Looks Like* (Ventura, CA: Regal Books, 1999), p. 160.

CHAPTER FIVE

"Closet" Prodigals

The LORD does not look at the things man looks at. Man looks at
the outward appearance, but the LORD looks at the heart.

—1 SAMUEL 16:7

My own church tended toward perfectionism, which tempted us
all to follow the example of Ananias and Sapphira in
misrepresenting ourselves spiritually. On Sundays well-scrubbed
families emerged from their cars with smiles on their faces even
though, as we later found out, they had been fighting abusively
all week long. . . . It never occurred to me that church was a place
to be honest. Now, though, as I seek to look at the world through

the lens of grace, I realize that imperfection is the prerequisite for grace. Light only gets in through the cracks.[1]

– PHILIP YANCEY

Outward appearances can be deceiving where prodigals are concerned. Their surface demeanor is such that few recognize they actually are prodigals. Some, like Esther, may not go to the "far country,"[2] but they grow cold toward the Lord in their hearts and drift away. Among family members and friends, someone usually sees the situation and begins to pray.

On the way to becoming the head of a successful business corporation, Esther became a "closet" prodigal because of discrepancies she saw in the lives of some Christians.

"The pastor of the church I grew up in preached a very harsh, legalistic message—telling people how they should live," she said. "Yet in his own home this man often had fits of rage and physically abused his wife and children. They would come to our house for refuge to escape his wrath. Such inconsistency between his public message and his private life made me very cynical about Christianity in general."

When Esther graduated from high school she wanted to enroll at a university, but her parents persuaded her to go to Bible school. They promised to pay her expenses to study for a degree in business administration if she would first attend Bible school, so she consented.

"I was there against my will, so of course I looked at everything in the most negative light," she said. "But the administration had the same legalistic views my pastor had upheld, and I saw enough hypocrisy in two years to further reinforce my cynicism."

Esther completed her secular education, got married and established a successful career. Because church had always been a part of her life, she joined an evangelical church. But her main purpose was to achieve success in business, gain approval of her peers and acquire all the rewards that worldly accomplishment can bring. Finding her business associates much easier to relate to than many Christians she knew, she attended church only on Sunday mornings and kept her distance by leaving early. But she had a close friend, Sonja, who was praying for her.

"Sonja is a sincere Christian whom I really respect," she said. "When she asked me to go with her to a nearby city to hear her mom speak at a seminar, I reluctantly agreed—and quickly wished I hadn't. But at the meeting, during the worship, I truly experienced God's presence in a profound way for the first time. Then when Sonja's mom talked, it seemed she was looking straight into my soul. I knew God was speaking to me about my heart issues and making me accountable for my own sinful attitudes. No longer could I justify my lack of commitment to the Lord by hiding behind the hypocrisy excuse—I had to admit I truly was in a sinful state."

When Esther repented for her hardness of heart and judgmental attitude, her thinking totally changed. Worldly success and all it could provide lost its appeal. God began showing her ways He wanted her involved in ministry instead of in the business world. Soon she quit her job and volunteered as an administrator and consultant for a major prayer ministry. Her many years in the business world are now a great asset to this organization.

"The change that came to my life was like a whirlwind," Esther says. "My business associates and friends are astounded, because now my number one priority is to please God and build His kingdom. It still bothers me to see inconsistencies in the church, but I realize these people are only human, and I can't judge them—that's for God to do. Becoming a God pleaser instead of a man pleaser or a self pleaser gives me great freedom."

By her own admission, Esther was a closet prodigal—perhaps not so different from many professing Christians who fill the pews of churches every Sunday morning but whose hearts are far from God. The reality that God is our Father means He wants a personal relationship with each one of us. And He makes that possible through His Son, Jesus.

Closet prodigals are everywhere. Many, like Esther, attend church regularly. One could say of them the same thing God said about the nation of Israel: "These people come near to me with their mouth and honor me with their lips, but their hearts are far from me. Their worship of me is made up only of rules taught by men" (Isa. 29:13).

> Closet prodigals are everywhere. Many professing Christians fill the pews of churches every Sunday morning, but their hearts are far from God.

Marlene, on the other hand, is an example of the people Jesus spoke of who hear the Word "but as they go on their way they are choked by life's worries, riches and pleasures, and they do not mature" (Luke 8:14).

She accepted Christ at age 12 and grew up in church with the support of a loving family. After earning a degree in pharmacy, she became a licensed pharmacist. Soon after moving to a large city and establishing a successful neighborhood pharmacy, she became engaged to Daniel, who was from a wealthy, influential family.

Guilty of Fraud

"In a short time it seemed I had it all—a beautiful home in an elite area, a Mercedes sports car, an extensive stock portfolio and a prominent fiancé," Marlene said. "Relying on these things for my security, I had left God out of my life. Daniel and I kept up appearances by attending church, paying tithes and supporting worthwhile causes. But without realizing it, I actually was perishing."

Though her parents were concerned about her materialistic lifestyle, they never confronted her—they simply prayed. Marlene's life quickly spiraled downward when she learned she was the object of an investigation by a federal prosecutor. Caught up with enjoying the benefits of her success, she had been negligent in overseeing her employees to be sure they followed government guidelines on a pharmaceutical contract she had won. When she and two employees were indicted, her livelihood and entire way of life suddenly was in jeopardy.

"My place of refuge was denial," Marlene says. "I refused to consider myself as a criminal or even to think about the possibility that I might go to prison—though the charge, if proven, called for a 5- to 10-year sentence in federal prison. I lived under the false illusion that my lawyers would find a way to get me out of this jam. The jury returned my verdict—guilty of fraud—and gave me a five-year sentence, to be followed by three years of supervised release. Yet my employees were acquitted."

About three weeks after Marlene went to prison, Daniel attended a home Bible study with a friend where he briefly shared what had happened to his fiancée and asked those in the group to pray for her. Afterward, a man from that group, Gary, felt God had instructed him to go visit Marlene in prison, even though he had never met her. It was like an Ananias and Paul scenario—God sending His emissary to pray for someone who had been blinded to "see again and be filled with the Holy Spirit" (Acts 9:17).

After driving three hours to find the prison, Gary went to the visitor's room and asked for Marlene. She came when the guard summoned her, expecting to see Daniel.

"Are you Marlene?" Gary asked. "My name is Gary, and God has sent me—can we go outside and talk?"

"I was suspicious at first," Marlene said, "but the fact that he knew my name got my attention. He seemed to have such a spiritual authority about him. We went out to a corner of the prison yard and he asked if I wanted to receive the Holy Spirit. In church I hadn't been taught about the Holy Spirit. 'Did God tell you to ask me that?' I asked. He said yes, and I allowed him to pray for me. When he did, I knew that something went out of me and something else came into me. Amazingly, no guards came around to investigate why a man was laying hands on an inmate—I believe the Lord blinded their eyes so that I would be set free."

A School of the Holy Spirit

After this experience, Marlene's life in prison became a school of the Holy Spirit as she studied God's Word and allowed Him to reveal how she had come into such bondage. Soon she was teaching Bible classes and ministering spiritual freedom to other inmates. Though prison was a very difficult, demonic environment, for five years the Lord used it to teach her about the kingdom of God. Unknown to Marlene, God had a plan of true freedom in motion for her.

"Even in the midst of my rebellious, self-sufficient, prideful life, God never stopped pursuing me," Marlene said. "I know the prayers of my parents and others God called to pray for me are the key to my deliverance from the bondage that had so ruled my life."

About a year and a half into her five-year prison term, Daniel broke up with her and married someone else. But the Lord spoke to her through Joel 2:25: "I will repay [or restore] you for the years the locusts have eaten." She believed this meant that when she got out of prison her license would be reinstated, allowing her once again to work as a pharmacist. After all, this was the only means of livelihood she knew. When she surrendered her license upon going to prison, members of the board had seemed sympathetic with her case. Some even felt she should never have been convicted in the first place.

After her release, Marlene drove to the state capitol to meet with the licensing board to request reinstatement. While sitting in the reception room awaiting her turn, she prayed for the other pharmacists in the room who were going through a similar process. *Looks like this will be a shoo-in,* she thought as she observed several go in for their meeting one by one and then come out smiling. But when she walked into the boardroom, it was as if someone had just dumped ice water on the group of examiners. In effect, they put her on trial all over again and finally said she would not be licensed to practice pharmacy again.

She had already paid a huge fine that wiped out all her assets. Now this news left her numb with shock. Getting on the elevator to leave the building, Marlene got another surprise, moments later, when all the board members got on the same elevator with her. But she remembered how the Lord had taught her she must bless her enemies and not curse them, so she greeted them cordially. She even thanked them for their help when she left the elevator. Then she got in her car and reality set in, followed by anger.

"God, you promised to restore the years the locusts have eaten," she cried. "How am I going to make a living without my license?"

Without waiting for an answer, she drove to a restaurant where she was to meet friends for dinner, still feeling angry at God. During dinner no one asked about how her meeting went or showed any interest in her personal concerns, which further upset her. But afterward, a man in the group privately handed her a check which more than provided for her immediate needs.

"God made it very clear to me that my pharmacy license was not my source—He is my source for everything I need," Marlene said. "During the period of my supervised release, I've worked in various positions for an evangelistic ministry and a church. By getting the judge's permission, I've even been allowed to leave the country on short-term missions trips. Now that this period is almost over, I know God will guide me into areas of ministry I could never have imagined possible. Meanwhile, some of the women I taught in prison are continuing to teach the Bible to their inmates, just as I taught them."

"You Can Walk Back"

Marlene became a closet prodigal because she allowed her worldly success and possessions to crowd God out of her life. Sometimes being hurt and disappointed by other Christians' behavior causes a believer to pull away from the faith.

Iverna Tompkins describes a period when her life took a wayward turn because of disappointing relationships and hurt and disillusionment she felt while serving in a church staff position:

I experienced deep discouragement and ended up walking out of the church declaring, "If that is how they treat Christians, I want no part of it." Hurt and frustrated, I allowed bitterness and hatred to fill my heart for the first time in my life.

I began dating unbelievers and ultimately fell in love with one and married him. Life seemed easy for a while, but I was aware that something was missing. Although I often found myself witnessing to people in need, I had no prayer life, didn't read the Word and was always glad to share my bitterness about Christians.

It was during my pregnancy that I faced the truth and acknowledged that I needed God's help. I returned to church but felt nothing. My husband was overseas with the armed services, and although I attempted to regain my precious time with Jesus, I felt empty and alone.

One day I asked Him, "Why do I feel nothing?"

"You walked away; you can walk back," I heard Him say.

A new determination gripped me, and day after day I prayed and read my Bible. One day while driving to my job I heard myself declare, "I may never cry again or feel Your presence, but I will spend eternity with You because Your Word promises that!"

Tears flowed as though a dam had burst; joy replaced the barrenness I'd known. That experience has been a deterrent against backsliding through the years, and I have never ceased to be grateful for His presence.

I wish I could say that my marriage improved when I turned back to the Lord, but in fact it deteriorated. I lacked wisdom in sharing the changes that were taking place in me, and my husband and I found less and less interest in each other's lives. After 10 years of marriage, and following the births of my daughter and son, he left one final time.[3]

Today Iverna is a respected spiritual leader who ministers hope and encouragement to those struggling with despair because of their past failures. "Nothing you have done—no mistakes you have made—can disqualify you," she says.

As Iverna learned, the Lord wants to whisper to many closet prodigals, "You can walk back." And like the prodigal in Jesus' story, they can begin their pilgrimage home.

Living with a Closet Prodigal

Each of us must be on guard so that disappointing circumstances don't pull us away from an intimate relationship with the Lord. But what should our response be when we become aware that someone close to us is living a lie—that he or she is, in effect, a closet prodigal?

Kerrie had to deal with this very issue when she realized her minister husband, Walter, had a public face and a private face, and they looked nothing alike. Outwardly he came across as a dedicated, self-sacrificing minister who wanted to reach inner-city youth with the message of Jesus' love for them. But in private he was controlling, abusive and dishonest. Kerrie had accepted the Lord as a young teenager in camp, and Walter was her youth pastor. Since he was eight years older and Kerrie had no Christian background whatsoever, she tended to accept whatever he said as being right.

After they were married, Walter's behavior became increasingly disturbing, and she learned he was indulging in pornography. She confronted him with evidence she'd found that he was having an affair, but he denied it, so she presented the evidence to the pastor over them. Although he fired Walter, the pastor chose to keep the firing and the adultery issue quiet. For him, this was easier than trying to deal with the problem.

Kerrie left Walter for a period of time, but when he promised to change she believed him. Then they moved to another city and established their own ministry for children and youth. But Walter's deceitful ways went with them.

Now that he was no longer accountable to a close associate, he pretty much lived as he pleased. Kerrie would refuse when he wanted her to lie about the church finances or about his physical condition when a feigned injury or illness would increase his money-raising appeal. Her unwillingness to cooperate infuriated him.

While she was pregnant, Kerrie suspected Walter was having affairs with young women in their ministry, but she had no way to prove it at the time. After their daughter's birth the situation only worsened.

Kerrie never wanted a divorce. She wanted Walter to be discipled by an older, wiser man so he could minister with integrity in the work they had established together. She appealed for help from a minister in another city who was supposed to have oversight of Walter's work. But when a committee of ministers called him in for an interview, they believed his story that Kerrie was "burned out" with the pressures of ministry and had falsely accused him out of spite. Her only recourse was to pray and ask for God's intervention and direction.

When their little girl was three years old, Walter moved out of the house and got an apartment near the ministry center. He did provide minimal financial support for Kerrie but would try to control her by sending the check late or not at all and by threatening to withdraw his support altogether. Then he filed a divorce/custody suit, making many false accusations against her.

Kerrie knew she needed to forgive Walter for all the ways he had hurt and disappointed her or she never would be able to go on with her life. She tried to make excuses to God, such as, "If I forgive him, he can hurt us again or I would be approving of his sin." Finally she prayed, "Lord, I don't know how to forgive a person who did what he did and still continues to treat us like he does. But You said to forgive, so I choose to obey. You will have to help me." Once she crossed that hurdle, she walked in greater peace and confidence than she had known for years.

God continued to intervene for Kerrie in miraculous ways, and when the divorce finally was settled, the courts ruled in her favor. She was able to go to college in order to find a decent job and take care of her daughter. "The night I chose to forgive Walter, the Lord took a heavy burden off my back," she said. "I didn't know it was there until it was gone. I thought forgiveness was a gift to an abuser, but it was freedom for me. God has never failed us, and I know He never will."

To date, Walter still is a closet prodigal. He has not taken responsibility for any of his wrongdoing, yet he continues in public ministry as if nothing is wrong. Many of his staff members have left because of his dishonest dealings and have apologized to Kerrie for believing the lies Walter told about her. Kerrie continues to put the matter in God's hands, knowing that she is only responsible for her own actions and attitudes. But she is free from the bondage of bitter judgments and unforgiveness, and safe in God's abundant provision.

"God Always Has a Plan"

Victor, a popular young man and leader in his church, became a closet prodigal because he indulged in a secret sin until it controlled him. His mom, Maggie, and her husband believed that if they trained their son in God's ways as a child, he would not turn away from the truth when he grew older (see Prov. 22:6). And they tried to practice it. Victor received Christ at age 12, and a year later was baptized.

"During his teen years, we felt the Lord mercifully kept Victor from evil influences," Maggie told us. "He seemed to be able to rightly divide the Word of truth and to convey it to others. By the time he was in his early 20s he sometimes shared the pulpit on Sunday mornings and he also taught the youth at summer camps and served often on the mission field."

At age 26, Victor married. He and his wife had three beautiful children. God blessed him with a prosperous business, and he was a generous giver. On the surface, all appeared to be righteous in his life. But unknown to family and friends, Victor had allowed pornography to get a grip on his life when he was 15. Eventually this evil habit began to control him.

When his secret sin was openly exposed, Victor began drinking, taking drugs and having affairs. His wife left him, his business failed and close relationships with people he loved were broken. He became so mentally unstable that he was hospitalized, then placed in a rehabilitation center. Some claimed he was unreachable.

But Maggie, along with many of her friends, was praying, fasting and clinging to God's promises concerning her son. "In reality, no amount of counseling—no intervention on our part— seemed to help," she said. "We appeared powerless. But God always has a plan, and His plan is always powerful."

About that time, a childhood friend of Victor's went to his rehabilitation center and got permission to take him to his home. For more than a year this friend and his wife took responsibility for Victor, treating him as a member of the family.

"Finally, my son returned to his right mind," Maggie says. "He called upon the Lord and expressed deep repentance for his behavior. His relationships with his wife and children, age 5, 10 and 14, are being restored. Though he and his ex-wife haven't yet remarried, he does see the children regularly. His business is being rebuilt and he's considering going on short-term missions trips again. It has been a long, hard battle, but I rejoice to see how God is working in his life."

A Dual Lifestyle

Closet prodigals often experience a turnaround completely on their own, simply because the Holy Spirit convicts and pursues them.

In an article in *Christianity Online Magazine*, author Max Lucado told of his high school years when he, in his words, "walked the path of the prodigal" but kept it hidden from his parents. He said, "During that stretch, I probably abandoned every single value that I'd been taught. I'd go to church, but I would not listen. I wouldn't sing. I led a dual life."

The pattern continued after he enrolled at a Christian college. But when he took a required course on the life and teachings of Christ, he began to see Jesus in a different light. Shortly thereafter, a local preacher's radio sermon made a tremendous impact on him. "All I remember was that he was saying why Jesus died on the cross. . . . It caused me to pull over to the side of the road and say, 'Hey, God, I'll give my life back to you.' "[4]

This former prodigal went on to complete a theological degree and then serve as a missionary in Brazil. Today he is a respected minister and author whose inspirational books have blessed millions of people. "When I start feeling cocky, I look back at where I'd be without God's grace," he said.[5]

Yes, there is hope for closet prodigals.

A biblical example of a dual-lifestyle individual is King David, when he committed adultery with Bathsheba and then had her husband murdered to disguise the sin (see 2 Sam. 11). God sent the prophet Nathan to challenge David, "Why did you despise the word of the LORD by doing what is evil in his eyes?" (2 Sam. 12:9). The confrontation brought repentance.

If someone really close to us—such as a spouse, a child or a sibling—is a closet prodigal, we need to make sure we have clear guidance from the Holy Spirit before confronting him or her. Such individuals are walking in deception, so they often won't respond to reason or acknowledge their need for repentance. But we can pray that their spiritual eyes will be opened and make sure we don't harbor unforgiveness against them. It could be that we are the very instrument God wants to use to set them free.

Prayer

Lord, help me to guard my own heart that I don't get embittered by pain and disappointment. I want my life to shine as a bright light for You so others will desire to know You personally. No more charade for those precious ones I've been praying for. Lord, they hear the Word preached from the pulpit from time to time. Let Your words penetrate, Spirit to spirit. Forgive me for turning them away by my often unkind judgments. Amen.

Questions to Think About

1. How can I express my love and concern for them in creative ways? Have I ever been a closet prodigal—keeping up outward appearances but turning away from God in my heart?

2. Am I guilty of being too quick to judge others—including my prodigal—by outward appearances?

Notes

1. Taken from *What's So Amazing About Grace?* by Philip Yancey. Copyright © 1997 by Philip D. Yancey. Used by permission of Zondervan Publishing House, p. 248.

2. Luke 15:13, *NKJV.*

3. Iverna Tompkins, "When We Wander from God," *SpiritLed Woman* (October/November 1999), pp. 50, 51.

4. Randy Bishop, "Simply Max," *Christianity Online Magazine,* 2000. http://www.christianity.net/cr/2000/001/1.18.html (accessed January 27, 2000).

5. Ibid.

CHAPTER SIX

Prodigal Parents

No ear has perceived, no eye has seen any God besides you,
who acts on behalf of those who wait for him.

—ISAIAH 64:4

When we intercede for others we are engaging in battle
on their behalf. And most interestingly, sometimes the
victory we win in prayer on behalf of others actually
has a way of returning to us as a blessing![1]

—DICK EASTMAN

Usually we think of a prodigal as being a son who yields to peer pressure and strays from the Christian values he grew up with. Or a daughter who marries an unbeliever and abandons her childhood faith. But sometimes the prodigal is one or both parents who choose not to walk in God's ways.

For many years, Jane had prayed for her father's salvation, with no outward evidence of any change of his heart. But she maintained her contact with him and kept on praying. Then she received word he was in the hospital and not expected to live. She shares her story:

When we arrived at the hospital we were shocked to see that Daddy's stroke had paralyzed his right side and he could not speak. He tried, but could only mumble. Embarrassed and not wanting us to see him like that, he waved his arm for us to leave.

Daddy was a nature lover and an avid reader—a very humble man, though he claimed to be an agnostic. My sisters and I and our families adored him, but he just had no interest in committing his life to the Lord.

Now he was in intensive care, and the doctors said he had only a few hours, or at the most a few days, to live. As we kept a vigil at the hospital, I wondered how we could get him to yield his heart to Christ.

On Sunday afternoon we called a local pastor to come pray for him. As he started to pray, Daddy jerked his head slightly, so we knew there was some response. The pastor continued by praying a beautiful prayer, thanking God that Jesus died for Daddy and desired to save him.

"I believe your father heard that prayer," the pastor said as he left. "Be assured we will continue praying for him tonight, and I'll be back to visit."

That evening I felt so defeated I couldn't stop crying. All the years of witnessing to our father and praying for him seemed hopeless. Our precious Daddy was going to face eternity without God.

Then I realized the enemy of our soul was there and that we were in spiritual warfare. My sister started reading Scriptures aloud over Daddy. With one hand on his shoulder, she read aloud for hours from a book filled with God's promises. As she stopped to rest, I sensed a real anointing of the Holy Spirit and I started to sing. I sang and prayed that Daddy would see Jesus— not us. I believe the Lord was doing a work in Daddy's heart as we sang, prayed and read.

It occurred to me that after 73 years of walking in his own way, he should be shedding tears of repentance. I asked the Lord for a sign that Daddy was hearing and believing. Moments later my sister and I watched with joy as we saw tears roll out the corner of his eye. We began praising the Lord because we believed Daddy had responded to Jesus' invitation. At about five o'clock in the early hours of a Monday morning, God's peace descended upon us. Somehow we just knew that Daddy was saved. The victory belonged to Jesus.

Over the next few days my sister continued to read Scriptures over Daddy, but now we were limited to 10-minute visits every hour. Later we learned that the thinking part of his brain was still functioning, though he seemed to be unconscious. That enabled him to hear the Word of God and accept Jesus. We knew that though the outer man was perishing, the inner man was growing as he heard the Word night after night. His countenance changed and he was more peaceful.

Then a few days before he died, Daddy opened his eyes and smiled—another sign to us that he had received the gift of salvation. He lived only 12 days after having the stroke, but during those days God was faithful to answer years of prayer for our father.

Workers in the Harvest

We know that God is not reluctant to save sinners, but Jesus did give these instructions: "The harvest is plentiful, but the workers are few. Ask the Lord of the harvest, therefore, to send out workers into his harvest field" (Luke 10:2). Prayer is not simply asking God to save the lost, but it is also praying that He will send out workers who will love them, share the gospel with them and bring them to Christ. As volunteers in His harvest field, we need to be sensitive to the Holy Spirit's leading as He uses us to help answer someone else's prayers for a loved one. Let me share with you a time when the Lord scheduled such a divine appointment for me:

One morning a phone call from my son interrupted my (Quin's) busy schedule. "Mom, my roommate's mother is dying of throat cancer in a military hospital near you," he said. "He has recently accepted Jesus, but he's concerned because, as far as he knows, his mother doesn't know the Lord. Would you go see her and maybe pray for her?"

I revised my schedule for that day and asked my prayer partner, Fran, to join me in this visit to a stranger. When we walked into the room, Beatrice was in such pain she could barely talk. Much of the bone in the left side of her face had been removed, and she was surrounded with tubes and gauges and medical equipment. She did manage a weak smile when we introduced ourselves.

"Did you know your son Mickey has become a Christian?" I asked, getting right to the point of our visit. "My son rooms with him and has seen such a happy change in him. In fact, Mickey is concerned about your spiritual condition."

"Yes, he told me; I'm glad for him," Beatrice said. "I used to go to church when I was little, but I haven't been there in years. I still remember the old hymns we sang. But I've turned my back on God all these years . . . it's just too late for me."

Fran picked up the conversation, assuring her it was not too late. "Jesus will accept you right where you are," she urged. "Just ask Him to forgive your sins and tell Him you want to become His child forever."

As Fran read her several Scripture verses, I prayed silently. Finally Beatrice said, "I'm ready to ask Him to forgive me and be my Savior and Lord." We listened as she whispered a prayer, "Lord Jesus, please forgive me for my rebellion . . . for running from You. Come live in my heart. I want to be Yours."

I visited her a few more times, taking her a Bible and some Christian literature. I always prayed aloud with her before I left. Beatrice grew too weak to talk, but she could still squeeze my hand when I prayed with her.

She died within a few weeks. At the funeral home I met her son Mickey. "She accepted Jesus before she died," I told him. "I heard her whispered prayer with my own ears. She was so happy you have become a Christian."

I'd hardly finished my sentence when an elderly lady spoke up. "Forgive me for listening in, but I'm Beatrice's mother. I taught Sunday School for 40 years, and I can't remember a day when I didn't pray for my prodigal child—my only daughter—to come back to the Lord."

"Well, dear, your prayers were answered," I said.

"She made it to heaven!" the woman exclaimed, wiping tears

from her eyes. "She actually accepted Jesus just days before she died! Thank You, Jesus! Thank You, Lord, for Your faithfulness."

I left the funeral home thanking the Lord for the opportunity to be a part of the answer to the prayers of that mother and son.[2]

Any Unfinished Business?

When Jenny gave her heart to the Lord as an adult, she longed for her elderly mother to know Jesus, too—not just attend church on Easter and Christmas. "I hadn't been a reliable or trustworthy daughter, so I had to prove myself," she told me. "Mother needed to see that Jesus Christ had really changed my life before she would be willing to follow my example."

Jenny and her husband decided they would show love and forgiveness toward her at every opportunity. Then her mother agreed to enroll in a Bible course with Jenny and they grew much closer.

After Jenny's father died, her mom began to lean on her more and more. A short time later she committed her life to the Lord, and the two began relating to one another in a fresh and deeper way. When the mother faced open-heart surgery, they both realized she might not live through it.

"The day before her surgery I spent the entire day with her in her hospital room," Jenny said. "I asked if she had any unfinished business with God or if she needed to forgive anyone. For hours Mom unburdened her heart. Each time a new topic of hurt surfaced we stopped and prayed about it. She talked through some very pain-filled areas of her life, some regrets and disappointments. As I prayed over each area, she and I both experienced a supernatural joy unlike anything we had ever known."

Her mother lived 15 more months after the surgery. During this time God provided a support group of praying friends for Jenny and good medical care for her mom. "It is never too late for someone to come into the Kingdom," Jenny declared.

A Child Calling
the Parent to Repentance

When God gave the Law to Moses, He also instructed the people to teach His precepts to their children and explain how God had delivered them from the slavery of Egypt. The natural progression is for the older generation to instill spiritual truth and values in the younger generation. But when the parents disobey God or turn away from Him, He may use the children to speak truth to their elders.

One example of this is Gideon. Because the nation of Israel had disobeyed God by worshiping idols, He allowed their land to be occupied and ravaged by the cruel Midianites. When the people cried out to God, he sent an angel to commission the young man Gideon to strike down Israel's enemies. But first he had to tear town the altar to Baal that his father had built. When that was done, God gave Gideon victory in defeating the Midianites (see Judg. 6,7).

When the parents disobey God or turn away from Him, He may use the children to speak truth to their elders.

Another example is Samuel and his spiritual father, Eli the priest. Eli had allowed his natural sons to defile the tabernacle. God spoke through the boy Samuel to warn Eli that He would judge his family because of this sin (see 1 Sam. 3).

In both cases, the younger generation addressed the sin of the older generation in order to see God's blessing come upon the land. Sometimes that pattern is repeated today.

Returning to the Fold

Jesus said, "The thief comes only to steal, and kill, and destroy; I came that they might have life, and might have it abundantly" (John 10:10, *NASB*). It seems that the enemy of our souls is especially bent on stealing a family's spiritual heritage. But God can empower us to reclaim the ground the enemy has stolen from us.

After becoming a Christian as an adult, Sondra learned that her father had grown up in a Christian home. But his faith didn't stand the test of his military service during World War II, and he had instilled no godly values in his children as they were growing up. Then he joined a humanistic, non-Christian group. Sondra began praying that the Word sown in his heart many years ago would speak to him and that he would return to the faith of his fathers.

"When I received Christ, my parents noticed the changes in me—especially when I was healed from years of chronic asthma and allergies," she said. "Dad showed no outward evidence of change or any interest in my faith in God, but I remained steadfast in prayer. Then one day I felt the Lord told me to change my praying from supplication to thanksgiving—that the thing I'd prayed for was accomplished.

"I got a picture of my father lying in a single bed next to a dark wall. I was sitting at his right side and light was streaming in over my left shoulder. I didn't understand what it meant, but for two years I continued offering thanks to the Lord for His completed work. Then my father allowed me to pray for him when he had a gall bladder attack."

The following year he had a massive stroke. Sondra went to the hospital and found him lying in bed with a dark blue wall behind him—just as she'd seen during prayer more than two years earlier. The next morning she arrived very early and sat by her father's bed praying quietly as he slept.

"When a nurse came in to pull back the divider curtain and the drapes, the early morning sun streamed into the room, awakening him. I spoke to him gently, 'Dad, it's time for you to get right with God.' He nodded, and I led him in prayer. With tears streaming down his face, he grabbed me with his good arm and hugged me tightly.

"A few weeks later, while I was working in the kitchen, a familiar voice spoke to my heart. *Are you comforted, knowing that your father's life is in My hands?* Of course my answer was yes. Less than an hour later my husband arrived with the news that my father had died. Now he literally was in my Father's hands. Though it took many years, and the outcome wasn't just as I'd hoped, seeing the reconciliation of man to God is worth persevering in prayer."

Stand Up for Jesus

We've often encountered young people who are zealous to serve the Lord in full-time ministry, only to face tremendous opposition from one or both parents. In Karen's case the conflict caused years of alienation from her father because she determined to obey God's call. She shares her story:

Although I grew up attending my mother's church and learned about Jesus, I didn't truly know Him. My father went to please my mother, despite his very different Ukrainian background, but I doubt he understood the meaning of true commitment to Christ. Though he rarely showed much outward emotion, I knew by the little things Dad did for us that he truly loved me and my siblings.

One of my early memories is of him bathing us, one after the other, on the only evening of the week he didn't have to go to work for his night-shift mechanic's job. He would lift me out of the tub, stand me on the toilet seat, and dry me off while singing, "Stand up, stand up for Jesus, ye soldiers of the cross. Lift high the royal banner, it must not suffer loss." Then he would wrap me in a towel and send me off to put on my pajamas. Little did we know the day would come when I would have to choose to stand up for Jesus in opposition to my father's desires for my future.

At age 18 I received Jesus Christ as my Savior. When I got off my knees with tears of repentance running down my face, I knew Jesus had died for me and I was born again. A few months later I invited my whole family to attend my water baptism. Mom rejoiced with me, but since I had been baptized at age 12, Dad couldn't understand. My explanation fell on deaf ears, and he stayed home from the service.

I was working at a hospital and training to become a food service supervisor, but I knew God had more for my life and I wanted it. I learned about a Bible school in a nearby city and enrolled right away. Those were glorious days of soaking up the Word of God under the anointing of the Holy Spirit.

Visiting home during one of the breaks, I excitedly told my parents about the things I was learning. My father looked me straight in the eye and said sternly, "Don't you be getting fanatic about all this and become a missionary." His voice was fearful and tinged with anger as he spoke the very thing that soon would happen in my life. Pain struck my heart at his words, but the moment passed without incident.

At the end of my first year of school, I went on a ministry trip that took our team around the world—a unique opportunity for one as young as I was to see the needs of the world up close. It was in India that God spoke clearly to my heart that this was where I was destined to serve.

During my second year of studies, I sought the Lord in prayer and fasting for His guidance. One day toward the end of that year, the placement office called to say a request had come from an elderly missionary in India who needed help with her orphanage and school. I wrote her to volunteer, and the reply came by telegram: "WELCOME. COME!" As I began preparing to go, God put it in the heart of a dear friend to accompany me. He also provided the finances for both of us to go.

Though I was excited about going to India, I was in much prayer about telling my parents. When I arrived at the house, Dad was in the garage working. I went out to talk with him and told him I felt called to ministry and that I planned to go to India. He could see no sane reason for such a decision.

"God does not want you to do this," he declared. "God does not talk to us like this." It was a battle of the spiritual versus the natural—he simply could not understand. My heart was broken and grieved; his heart was broken and angry. It was the first battle of many to be fought.

Obeying God's Call

Karen went to India in obedience to God and spent three years there and in Sri Lanka, mainly involved in children's ministry. She faithfully wrote home to inform her parents of her well-being and the joy she had in serving the Lord. Her mother responded, but not her father. After three years she returned home to seek God's direction for the next step in her life; she stayed on the Bible school campus with a close friend.

When she went to visit her family, she arrived to find her father at home alone, preparing to go to work. They sat down in the living room to talk and she told him about all she had been doing in India. That was well and good, but he was more interested in what she was now going to do. "I expect to be in full-time ministry, Dad," she told him. "God has placed a special love and burden in my heart for India. I want to return and serve the Lord there."

"Don't do this to your life," he begged. "Don't spoil your life. You will have no future or happiness, and it is sheer madness." Again he was reacting with frustration and anger.

Then he challenged her: "Karen, what do you want? I will give you whatever you want. What school do you want to attend? I'll send you to the finest school. I'll give you a car. I'll do whatever you want and give you whatever you need, but please don't do this."

Oh, what a battle! In her heart she prayed, *I would do anything for You, Father, but this I cannot do. Oh, Lord, is there no other way? He doesn't understand. He loves me and I love him. Why do I have to break his heart? I don't want to hurt him. Is it right?*

Those words echoed in her mind—*Is it right? Is it right? Is it right?*

But Lord, I cannot deny You. Never had she felt so torn, yet so helpless.

Her father picked up his lunch box and left that day without another word, slamming the door behind him.

"I was a broken person," Karen said. "To him I was a prodigal because I obeyed God's call on my life. At the time, I had no idea that almost 20 years would pass before I'd see him again."

Over the next months she stayed on campus, attending some classes and visiting friends who had supported her through their prayers and gifts. During those days of seeking God's direction, she met her husband-to-be, an Indian national who had come to the Bible school under a work scholarship program. God brought them together and confirmed through many counselors that their marriage was in His plan.

Karen says, "When we decided to marry, my fiancé contacted his parents and received their blessing. I in turn called my father to tell him my decision, but I knew there would be no blessing. This was the final breaking point in our relationship. In a rage he said, 'I never want to see you again. You are dead as far as I am concerned. In fact, don't even come to our city again. Leave this country and don't return.' "

Karen's mother told her that from that day he would not allow her name to be spoken in their home. All photographs of her were taken down and the topic was never discussed. "My dear mother bore a heavy cross during those years. When I realized the heartache I caused my parents, it seemed as if God was requiring too much from me. Yet I knew if I obeyed God's call He would take care of my family."

The day after the wedding, they left for India. Karen has served the Lord there along with her husband and his family for almost 20 years. Her first three years were times of tremendous adjustment; also her daughter, Emily, was born there.

"When Emily was three years old, the two of us returned home for a visit," Karen reported, "but my father refused to see us. I returned to India with a heavy heart, praying, *Lord, not my will but Thy will be done.*

"In those days of testing the Lord spoke comfort to me through Scripture."

The Walls of Alienation Come Down

The story does not end there. As Emily was growing up, Karen promised to take her to America to meet her grandparents and family when she finished her 10th year of school. Here's what she told us:

I set that date with God and humbly requested Him to meet it. After 13 long years, Emily and I left India again to visit various places in Europe, and finally to the U.S. The Bible school I had attended provided accommodations, and it was a haven of rest for us.

My mother was longing to see us, but for me the thought of telling my father of our visit seemed like a dark tunnel with no light at the end. I could only leave everything in the Lord's hands. I even resigned myself to the possibility of not seeing my father at all. There was a great silence in my life during those days—this is the only way I can describe it. Then, at my sister's invitation, we packed up and moved to her home in a nearby city.

"Daddy is going to meet you and Emily," she said when I arrived. My brother had come from Georgia and talked with our father, and he had agreed to see us. At last the morning of our reunion arrived.

The minute my father came through the door I literally saw a puff of smoke go up into the air and disappear. It was as if the walls of Jericho came down when he reached out and hugged me with tears running down his face. We cried, and I said, "Daddy, I love you. Please forgive me." What an unforgettable experience. It was as though all those years of pain had never existed. Our conversation was only of the present. While spending the remaining days with my parents, I saw my daughter visibly changed by the great acceptance and love my father showered upon her. Each moment was so precious for me.

On the day we were leaving to return to India, the whole family gathered at the airport. I was sitting next to my father, and I will never forget his words.

"Do you remember the things I said when I last spoke to you?" he asked. "Well, I want you to forgive me."

It broke my heart, and I wanted to put my finger to his lips. "No, Daddy, it's not you who should ask me for forgiveness—it is I who should ask you," I said. "Forgive me for all the heartache I have caused you."

It was enough. And with a last embrace before entering the plane, I committed my father into the hands of the Good Shepherd.

I cannot say for sure that my father is born again or that he yet understands the call on my life. But I am confident that the God who brought reconciliation and healing between us will fully reveal Himself to this man who loves me in a new and deeper way.

The Old Versus the New

In cultures with no Christian background whatsoever, such as those in Asia, often the young people are the first to respond when they hear the gospel proclaimed. A conflict with the older generation usually follows.

I (Ruthanne) have a Chinese friend, Rosy, who was the first in her devout Buddhist family to receive Christ. The tradition in her family was for the parents to take her and her many siblings to the temple every week. They paid the Buddhist priests to write prayers and predictions of good luck for each of the children. The papers containing these writings were burned at an altar; then the ashes were stirred up in water and the children had to drink the mixture. The parents did this thinking it would assure the safety and well-being of their children. "The truth is, we actually were ingesting demons every week," Rosy told me.

At age 18, Rosy accepted an invitation to attend a Christian youth camp, mainly because she was interested in the young man who was the speaker for the camp. For the first time, she heard the message that Jesus Christ had died for her sins and made a way for her to find peace with God. Rosy accepted the Lord at that youth camp, and the young evangelist ended up becoming her husband.

She eagerly studied the Bible, memorized Scripture and began praying for her immediate family to receive Christ. At first they completely rejected Rosy and her newfound faith, but gradually, one by one, they began responding to the gospel. Over several years she led every family member to the Lord. For many years she and her husband have been in full-time ministry, mostly in Asia, and now their son is preparing to do missions work among Muslims.

One Chinese church I know of hosts a special banquet each year for honoring one's father and mother. Church members are encouraged to bring their parents—especially those who are not believers. After years of intercession, my friend Helen saw her elderly Buddhist parents receive Christ after they were honored at one of these events. We can honor the gifts and talents of our parents, thanking God for the gift of life they gave us, even if they aren't (or weren't) believers.

Maybe we are the first generation of Christians in our families. If so, we have the privilege to be the first to stand in the prayer gap for them. We can be an example by loving them and diplomatically speaking to them of their spiritual needs as the Lord gives opportunity. Our ultimate goal is to see them respond to Jesus' invitation, "Come unto Me."

Prayer

Lord, I'm grieved because my parents have not yet become believers. I know it is not Your will that they perish. I stand in the prayer gap for them, asking for Your mercy, forgiveness and favor for them. Let Your Holy Spirit woo them to Jesus. Reveal Yourself to them in whatever way You wish—through me or another person, a dream, a book, a song, a sermon, a Christian television program. Father, I pray they don't die without making a decision to embrace Jesus as their Lord. I thank You for my parents. I honor them. Give me creative ways to express my love, appreciation and concern for their spiritual condition. Thank You in advance for reaching them. Amen.

Questions to Think About

1. Can I identify any godly influences in the lives of my prodigal parents for which I can be grateful?

2. Am I careful to honor them even when we don't agree and to try to relate to them with humility and unconditional love?

Notes

1. Dick Eastman, *Love on Its Knees* (Tarrytown, NY: Fleming H. Revell, 1989), pp. 31, 32.
2. From *How to Pray for Your Family and Friends* © 1990 by Quin Sherrer and Ruthanne Garlock. Published by Servant Publications, Box 8617, Ann Arbor, Michigan, 48017, pp. 110-112. Used with permission.

CHAPTER SEVEN

Prodigal Spouses, Siblings and Others

For he himself is our peace, who has made the two one and has destroyed the barrier, the dividing wall of hostility. . . . He came and preached peace to you who were far away and peace to those who were near.

—EPHESIANS 2:14,17

So often, the people whom we love but who are far away from God are those who have hurt us deeply. We need to make sure that we feel no resentment toward them as we pray for them.

It is possible to pray fervently and for many years
for people we have never forgiven. This is a major
hindrance to our prayers being answered.[1]

—JOY DAWSON

Spouses, brothers, sisters, aunts, uncles, nieces, nephews. Most of us have prodigal relatives whom God has given us as prayer assignments. Sometimes we pray for them for years—and when the miracle of salvation comes, it is through someone else.

Quin's Aunt Betty prayed daily for 19 years for her husband, Daniel, to accept the Lord. She never gave up believing that someday he would, but she didn't let his lack of faith stop her from going to church alone.

"When the light goes out, that's all there is to life," he'd say when Betty tried to get him—a salty ex-Navy man—to think about what comes after death.

"No, it isn't," she would answer. "We all have a spirit that will live forever, and Jesus wants to give you eternal life with Him."

One autumn they needed a tree chopped down on their land in rural Oregon. Daniel's friend, Lee—once his drinking and fishing buddy—offered to come do it. Daniel noticed that Lee had changed drastically since he'd recently "gotten religion." Lee was a professional lumberjack and said he'd fell the tree for a promise from Daniel to attend church with him just one time.

Lee took care of the problem tree; then Daniel asked to have a second tree taken out. "You haven't paid me for the first one,"

Lee reminded him. So Daniel agreed to go to church with him the following Sunday. Betty gladly went along, though it wasn't the church she usually attended.

At that service, Daniel was moved to tears and began the process of surrendering his life to Christ. A few days later he was down at the creek below their house when he had a supernatural encounter with Jesus. Was it a vision? An angel? A voice from heaven? Daniel never described it in full detail. But when he came up the hill to the house, Betty found him pale and shaking all over.

Praying until change comes takes commitment and humility. And sometimes the one praying has to be willing to change.

"Something has happened to me. Hurry—come kneel and pray with me," he begged. Betty ran to the phone and called a missionary couple to come over. For two hours the four of them knelt in prayer as God dealt personally and privately with Daniel. Afterward he gave public testimony in church about his supernatural experience by the creek.

From that day in October until December, he never missed a service. But before the new year rolled around, Daniel had a heart attack and met his Savior. Betty's grief was tempered by the assurance that her Daniel was in heaven. The prayers she had prayed since the day they were married were answered.

Praying for an unbelieving spouse until change comes takes commitment and humility. And sometimes the one praying has to be willing to change.

A Prodigal Spouse

Bob and Annette are a classic example of the popular saying "Opposites attract." When they married, he was a macho Marine captain who placed a high priority on efficiency and frugality. Annette was a fun-loving redhead who was always the life of the party. She rarely formed lasting relationships—if problems arose, she just moved on to a new set of friends. It was no surprise that her first marriage failed when her son was quite young.

Bob was drawn to Annette's outgoing personality; she married him for stability and security. But when Bob tried to organize their home like a military camp—complete with detailed timetable— Annette rebelled against being treated like a Marine recruit. The stability and security now seemed rigid, opinionated and judgmental. They joined a church, but when the marriage became chaotic, their church offered no genuine spiritual help. Feeling that all the fun had gone out of her life, Annette filed for divorce.

Bob was devastated. No one else in his entire family had ever divorced, and to him it spelled failure. He attended a Christian men's meeting and went forward for prayer for his troubled marriage. He also accepted Jesus as Lord of his life.

However, the situation with Annette grew worse. His mother said, "Bob, you are both young and you can rebuild your lives. Go ahead and give Annette the divorce. You deserve some happiness."

"Mom, what would you think if I told you I was divorcing Annette because she had cancer and could no longer make me happy?" he asked.

"I would think you're terrible!" she said.

"Well, Annette has something worse than cancer—she has cancer of the spirit. Christ calls me to do more than seek my own happiness and personal well-being. I'm going to pray and believe

God to heal her spirit and restore our marriage."

For two years Bob tried to woo Annette back. He'd say to her, "I love you," and she would scream, "I hate you!" He didn't always handle her outbursts gracefully, but he began to see himself as her servant instead of her master. He said, "Annette, the devil is trying to destroy our home, but I'm going to love you and fight for our marriage for the rest of my life."

Annette committed her life to Jesus when she at last admitted she needed Him to fill the void in her life. Her hard heart melted as she responded to Bob's unconditional love, and God restored their marriage. Today the two are popular speakers for marriage retreats and they have an effective counseling ministry.[2]

The Bible gives an account of a husband with a straying wife in the book of Hosea. Gomer, the unfaithful wife, said, "I will go after my lovers, who give me my bread and my water" (Hosea 2:5, *NKJV*).

God told Hosea He would put a hedge of thorns—a protective barrier—around her so that her lovers would lose interest in her. That's exactly what happened. Then her heart changed. Praying these verses can be an effective prayer strategy for a prodigal spouse or child—or anyone who strays as Gomer did:

> Therefore, behold, I will hedge up your way with thorns, and wall her in, so that she cannot find her paths. She will chase her lovers, but not overtake them; yes, she will seek them, but not find them (Hosea 2:6,7, *NKJV*).

She Wanted Her Brother Included

When Pam returned to the Lord from her wanderings, she felt compelled to take up the prayer mantle of her deceased mother and grandmother and intercede for her siblings. The five children were raised by a godly mother who, as Pam says, "stood on the Word that [promised] if she taught us the way of the Lord, when we were old we would not depart from it. Mother and Grandmother—both married to unbelievers—prayed for years for this household."

After their deaths, several of the children strayed. "We turned away from God big time," Pam said, "figuring we'd make it back in before the Lord called us home. But in the meantime Satan was making his bid to trap us in the world."

Pam's brother O'Brien was a special disappointment for her—once a staunch believer, now drawn into relationships with unbelieving women. Finally, while stationed in Asia, he married a Buddhist there. Pam was heartbroken when she got the news.

"I prayed and prayed and prayed," she said, "and fought the anger. I screamed into the heavenlies, 'God, what about my mother's prayers? My grandmother's? How could You let this happen? My brother has embraced a false god!'"

Finally she came to a place of intercession that included repentance.

"I repented for every generational sin there was—telling God how sorry I was that our family had strayed. Then I asked God to remember the prayers of my grandmother and mother that were so powerful for us. For two years I fasted and prayed as the Lord led me. I was provoked to spiritual wrath. I would scream, 'Enough, enough, enough, Satan—my brother will not be robbed of his inheritance in God.'"

Pam became the head intercessor for a large men's ministry. One day she reminded God that she had prayed for hundreds of men and their families to be restored—and she wanted her brother included. A short time later, after an all-night prayer meeting with the ministry's staff, she barely had gotten back to her home when the phone rang. Happiness overflowed in her brother O'Brien's voice as he said, "Sis, I just wanted you to know I found the Lord—I've come home. I love Jesus, and I'm going to stay with the Lord. All the prayers for me were not in vain."

Soon after that, he came to visit Pam, bringing his Buddhist wife with him. Pam immediately took them to visit her spiritual mom, JoAnne. Before they left her house, JoAnne had led O'Brien's wife to Jesus. Today, three years later, Pam's brother and his wife are active members of a church.

Pam says she knew the Lord would keep His promises made to her mother and grandmother. She persistently reminded God that she was just adding her petitions to the prayers these two women had prayed long ago. The Lord spoke to her through Jeremiah 31:16,17 that her brother would return from the land of the enemy.

Overdosed at 35,000 Feet

When Gwen became a stepmother to Larry, she also became a prayer warrior for him. Her continuous prayer was, "Lord, do whatever You need to do to save him, but don't let him die." How close he came!

Larry had married a New Yorker who didn't like living in the South, so she'd gone back to New York. He went after her in one last effort to save the marriage. Feeling very depressed when she refused to return with him, he bought a supply of street drugs and took them with him on the airplane. After the plane reached an altitude of 35,000 feet, he ordered an alcoholic drink and swallowed the drugs with it. Immediately he got deathly ill, creating a crisis aboard the plane. The pilot considered making an unscheduled landing to save his life.

At his sickest moment, Larry cried out to God, "Save me! Oh, Lord, save me!" And a miracle happened. He was instantly healed and the flight continued on schedule. When the plane landed, not only was his physical health improved, but so was his spiritual condition. He came back to the Lord and eventually remarried and had two children.

Now his stepmother prays for God to give Larry strength and wisdom to live a righteous life. "I stood in faith for him so many years," she said. "Though he had to come to the end of himself while high in an airplane—when he literally could have died—yet God was merciful."

When I heard Gwen's story, I (Quin) was reminded of our pastor Dutch Sheets's teaching on "Tipping the Prayer Bowls of Heaven." He wrote about it in his book *Intercessory Prayer*:

Scriptures indicate that our prayers accumulate. There are bowls in heaven in which our prayers are stored. Not one bowl for all of them, but "bowls." We don't know how many, but I think it very likely that each of us has our own bowl in heaven. I don't know if it's literal or symbolic. It doesn't matter. [See Rev. 5:8; 8:3-5.] . . .

According to these verses, either when [God] knows it is the right time to do something or when enough prayer has accumulated to get the job done, He releases power. He takes the bowl and mixes it with fire from the altar.[3]

We can ask God to mix our prayers with those of the godly saints in our families who have gone before us, planting faith-filled prayers for the next generations.

Many Nights My Aunt Prayed for Me

The attractive blonde presiding over the women's meeting for which I (Quin) was to speak certainly didn't look like a prodigal. With her wide smile and pleasant demeanor, Paula looked nothing like the rebel she had been before her family's prayers—especially the prayers of her aunt—brought her back to the Lord. Later she wrote me the details of how God worked in her life.

I married at 15 and tried to be a Christian, pray and go to church, but it seemed I was married to the devil himself. My husband did everything to keep me from going to church. After 16 years of mental and physical torment from him, I felt God had abandoned me, so I ran away as far as I could—from God and from my husband.

First I tried to commit suicide by overdosing on drugs. Then I got involved in the occult and became a white witch—doing spells and telling fortunes. I looked for power in men and had a man for every need. While working in a go-go bar at night, I got hooked on crack cocaine and became an alcoholic. But I had a praying mother, aunt and sisters. Once my aunt told me that many nights the Lord awakened her to pray for me. "Someday you will have a wonderful testimony to share about Jesus' grace in your life," she said.

"You're crazy," I responded, knowing she had no idea of how deep in sin I had fallen. When I finally hit bottom, my daytime boss gave me an ultimatum. To keep my job I must either check into a rehab hospital or enroll in the Alcoholics Anonymous program. I did the latter.

At the meetings, when we were encouraged to seek the "higher power," I knew for me that was Jesus. I begged Him to forgive me. He not only forgave me, but He also delivered me from my addictions, from my occult involvement and from my need for illicit sex. I repented of all the things I'd done that were an abomination to Him.

For the past nine years I've been married to a wonderful Christian man who deeply loves the Lord and me. Now when members of my family have problems, they call me—once the black sheep of the family—to pray for them. I'm so grateful for my aunt's faithful prayers. Today I'm praying for my own prodigal daughter; I know He can reach her just as He reached me, no matter how far she strays.

A Friend Intercedes

Sometimes God puts thoughts of someone on your heart until you get so concerned about her spiritual life that you pick up a prayer burden for her. Fran did that for Ginger, though at first they weren't especially close friends.

Ginger hadn't been married to Fred long when she divorced him and took their little girl with her to California. Her parents persuaded her to return to Florida and finish college, agreeing to baby-sit for her.

Fran was also attending the college, and she and Ginger were in several classes together. They ended up carpooling for the 80-mile round-trip. On Ginger's day to drive, Fran would read the Bible—sometimes aloud. But soon Ginger would shout, "Shut that Bible or get out."

Sensing Ginger's wounded past, Fran shared how God had healed her own troubled marriage. She invited Ginger over for a meal to meet her husband, Mike. When Ginger expressed amazement at their devoted relationship, Fran simply said, "It's because Jesus Christ is the Lord of our lives."

Ginger often made fun of her ex-husband, Fred, who had become a committed Christian after the divorce. Inwardly, though, she was jealous of the peace Fred, Fran and Mike all seemed to have. One day, after one of her smart remarks about Fred, Fran said to her, "It sounds like Fred is happy since he's found the Lord—he certainly doesn't need you messing up his life."

Ginger drove the rest of the way home in angry silence. She couldn't stand the thought of Fred being happy and functioning well without her, especially when she was so miserable. That night she called Fred and told him she thought they should reconcile.

He told her later, when they met for dinner, "I'm a Christian now, and I hesitate to marry someone who isn't."

"I'm not a believer, Fred, but give me time," she replied.

"I can try to love you with God's love," he told her, "even though I don't have any feelings for you. But I have been praying for Kris to have a daddy . . ."

One month later, after counseling with Fred's minister, they remarried on a Sunday morning at the close of the worship service, with family and friends present. It was three years to the date since the divorce. Five-year-old Kris was in her parents' wedding.

In a few weeks the old problems were back—Ginger lashing out at Fred in anger and he storming out of the house. One morning after such a blowup, Ginger called Fran. "Our marriage is just the pits—nothing has changed. I'm desperate."

"Your marriage will stay in turmoil until you are willing to give your whole life to Jesus," Fran told her. "Your problems are spiritually based. You have tried every other avenue and nothing has worked. This is the only solution."

That morning, Ginger bowed her head and prayed, "Lord Jesus, take over my life. I surrender my all to you."

From that moment her life changed rapidly. When disagreements came, Fred would say, "Ginger, let's pray about it." They would kneel by the bed and pray. Ginger began attending the Bible study Fran started just for her.

God not only restored Ginger and Fred's marriage, but He also improved every aspect of it. They often counseled couples in their home. "What we had to offer was the glue that put our marriage back together," Ginger said. "That glue is a personal relationship with Jesus and having His love in our hearts."

Two years ago, after typing a Bible course paper for Fred, Ginger lay down on the sofa to rest. Fifteen minutes later, Fred found her dead from an undiagnosed ovarian tumor that had ruptured, taking her life before she'd even reached 50. I (Quin) lost a friend. She had prayed with me regularly at Fran's home every Monday morning for three years. And she often chauffeured me throughout the United States to my speaking engagements, serving also as my prayer partner on those ministry trips.

What a witness her life was of the transforming power of God!

A Prodigal Daughter-in-Law

Sometimes we find ourselves praying for in-law children who have become prodigals. Anna shared such a story with us. Her son Stan met Marie at a young-adult church group soon after they graduated from college. When they were married in the church where they met, it seemed to be a storybook start to a strong Christian marriage.

"My husband and I were happy and confident that God had put them together," Anna told us. "Marie's childhood had been quite unstable because of her mother's death, and an aunt and uncle had raised her. But we bonded quite well and had a loving mother-daughter relationship."

The first three years went well, and then Marie was expecting their first child. She became quite unhappy when Stan's military transfer moved them back East. They didn't get connected with a good church, and Stan's research work and study for a master's degree demanded a lot of his time and attention.

After their son was born, Marie was a doting mother and seemed happy when Anna would visit. But as time went on, Marie more openly aired her complaints about Stan's being so busy with his work. Soon after the baby's first birthday, Stan was called to active duty during the Desert Storm conflict. Marie was angry and felt he had put going to war ahead of her. Meanwhile, her friendship with Patty, another military wife, became increasingly important to her. This woman had no children, and she and Marie spent more and more time together on their own. Anna remembers:

After Stan returned from overseas duty, Marie immediately became pregnant again. Assuming my prayers for her were being answered, I went to help her when she came home from the hospital with their second son. A short time later she called and asked me to stay with the boys again while she and her friend attended a tennis match for three days. In my eagerness to be with my grandsons, I agreed to go, but I felt uneasy about the relationship between Marie and Patty. From the moment I arrived it seemed they were constantly on the phone discussing every detail of their trip, or else Patty was there at the house. My sense of revulsion grew more intense, but all I knew to do was pray.

In the next few years it became clear that Marie preferred her relationship with Patty over her marriage. After attending a Christian men's rally, Stan came home repentant and asked Marie to forgive him for putting his job ahead of his family. When he told her the dreams he had for their future together, Marie told him the marriage was over—that he was a failure and a divorce was imminent. Sure enough, Stan's attempts to reason with Marie failed. A divorce followed, and Marie got custody of the two boys. Patty also got a divorce and moved in with her.

Now the focus of Anna's prayers has changed. She prays for her son's adjustment to this disappointment and for the protection and well-being of her grandsons. It has been an intense battle for the grandparents to win visitation rights, but now they are able to see the children once a month. That means flying hundreds of miles at great expense, but Anna feels it's important to have some positive input into their lives.

Divorce and its aftermath are terribly traumatic, but she and her husband don't let their pain stop them from praying faithfully for everyone involved in the situation.

Another Relative Joins the Kingdom

When family members are totally resistant to the gospel, our prayers still can be effective in bringing change. I (Quin) had an elderly aunt who repeatedly told me all my life, "I don't want your religion. And don't you dare pray for me when I'm sick and dying." Last year, just before she turned 94, I flew out to visit her. During our first afternoon together, I was careful not to talk about the Lord because it made her so mad. But this time, as I was leaving, I got bold enough to give her a book I had coauthored with Ruthanne—*Prayers Women Pray*.[4] Near the beginning of the book is a prayer one can repeat to accept Jesus as Savior and Lord. I was taking a big chance of receiving another rebuke.

When I visited her the next day, she didn't mention the book until I started to leave and was walking toward the car. "I read your book last night," she called. "Liked it. In fact, I now have my reservation in the upper room," she said, pointing up toward the sky. "Send me some more books like that."

I couldn't believe I'd heard her correctly—heaven referred to as the "upper room." But my friend Fran, who was with me, assured me my aunt had actually said that.

My aunt later told my uncle she had read a book that gave her peace and she no longer feared death. Over the next few months I sent her more books. When I would call, she asked for still another book. I went to see her again a few months later. For the very first time in my life, she actually allowed me to pray aloud for her. My tears spilled down her back as I held her tight and prayed.

Soon afterward, she got sick. When death was imminent, my sister went to keep vigil by her hospital bed, praying aloud and reading the Bible to her. My aunt always wanted to live to see the year 2000. And she did, only to die a few days later. It had been less than a year since I'd given her the book and she made a decision for heaven. How glad I am that God softened her heart to receive Him!

No matter which prodigal relative God lays on our hearts, we must carry the prayer burden until we see results. I used to ask the Lord why my godly mother, who loved and served Him, died so much sooner than my aunt—her sister—who often made fun of us for our faith. He never answered. But now I think I know. He was giving my aunt an opportunity to make her decision for Him.

One woman who has no children told me she prays daily for 42 nieces and nephews on her husband's side of the family. She believes she may be the only one who stands in the prayer gap for them.

Some of us may be totally surprised when we get to heaven to see lost relatives for whom we prayed. Perhaps we provided the prayer coverage, while someone else was God's instrument to bring them into the fold. God is asking us to be faithful in our prayer assignment.

Prayer

Lord, use me to help repair communication breaches and mend broken relationships. Help me not to be a party to dissension and strife. I want to please You as well as be a good example to others. When the time is ripe for me to talk with my relatives about their need for Jesus, enable me to speak with Your wisdom. Please go before me and let the Holy Spirit prepare their hearts for the seeds I will sow. Let me not be so concerned with whom You use to draw them toward You, but may I be faithful to do my part. Lord, bring them in, one by one—I ask in Jesus' name. Amen.

Questions to Think About

1. How can I become a godly influence in the lives of these loved ones without being self-righteous, preachy or judgmental?
2. How can I express my love and concern for them in creative ways?

Notes
1. Joy Dawson, *Intercession: Thrilling and Fulfilling* (Seattle: YWAM Publishing, 1997), p. 43.
2. From *How to Pray for Your Family and Friends*, © 1990 by Quin Sherrer and Ruthanne Garlock. Published by Servant Publications, Box 8617, Ann Arbor, Michigan, 48107, pp. 48-50. Used with permission.
3. Dutch Sheets, *Intercessory Prayer* (Ventura, CA: Regal Books, 1996), pp. 208, 209.
4. Quin Sherrer and Ruthanne Garlock, *Prayers Women Pray* (Ann Arbor, MI: Servant Publications, 1998).

CHAPTER EIGHT

When They Don't Come Home

Because of the LORD'S great love we are not consumed,
for his compassions never fail. They are new every
morning; great is your faithfulness.

—LAMENTATIONS 3:22

As time passes and I occasionally feel lonely for my only son,
the Lord reminds me of the words He once spoke
to a friend in New York whose son had been killed:
"I have your son, and you have Mine."

—A MOTHER WHOSE SON DIED WITH AIDS

Sometimes when prodigals show no sign of repentance, parents face hard and difficult decisions. Let them come home? Forbid them to come home? Show unconditional love? Help them financially? Withhold finances?

Just today a phone call came from a woman with a prodigal. She told me she prays by declaring the promises from God's Word and waiting in faith for the day he will be back. "But in the meantime I must trust God that he will come home. The waiting is the hardest. Satan whispers his lies to me over and over that it is just too late—that God will never rescue him."

The Wait of Faith

Pastor Peter Lord speaks of the "wait of faith" that most of us experience in praying for prodigals. He mentions four things we learn from this waiting:

1. God's concept of time is different from ours.
2. God has bigger, better plans than we know to ask for.
3. The wait teaches us that we need others in the Body of Christ to support us.
4. The wait purifies our faith.[1]

Then he relates his own experience:

Some time ago I went out to lunch with one of my children for whom I was at the time in the wait of faith. In

the course of our conversation I asked him several questions. His answers indicated no change in some funda-
mental areas of his life, areas necessary not only for
walking with God but for living life successfully on this
planet.

Instead of turning to the Lord and asking Him to
reconfirm His promise and give me encouragement, I
centered on the appearance of things and became discouraged and depressed. I did not respond to my son as
a father with a strong, pure faith in God, but as a father
who had no faith that his child was going to be
redeemed. A meeting that should have been a positive
encounter of love, mercy and grace turned instead into
a temporary setback in our relationship. . . .

You can be sure I repented, but I also saw how flawed
and imperfect my trust in God for this situation really
was.[2]

We hear from many intercessors who are in a wait-of-faith
phase of life right now. Here are just a few examples:

- A mother prays for her son who has become very
  wealthy but has turned away from God and now is
  about to marry an unbeliever.

- A grandmother prays for her 21-year-old granddaugh-
  ter who is hooked on crack cocaine.

- A mother with only one son left learns he has abandoned his wife and children and is living with a
  much younger woman. She prays his heart will
  change.

- A wife discovers her husband is secretly living a gay lifestyle and prays he will repent and change—but the marriage fails and then he develops AIDS.

- An adopted daughter who grew up in church finds her birth mother, learns she's not a Christian and now carries a prayer burden for her salvation.

Sometimes when the prodigal repents just before death comes, there is no outward evidence that he has returned to the Lord. But in such cases, God often gives assurance that the person has made peace with Him.

A mother who faithfully interceded for her rebellious son got word he'd been killed in a motorcycle accident. She had seen no evidence of change in his life and now called on the Lord for comfort. The Lord spoke to her, *His heart was toward Me—don't judge by his outward appearance.* That gave her confidence that her prayers had not been in vain.

A wife who had prayed many years for her backslidden husband was notified that he had been murdered in a jewelry store robbery. She was distraught to think he had lost his life before making things right with God. A few days later, a woman who had walked up to the scene moments after the shooting called her. "I realized what had happened and began to pray for the victim lying on the floor," she said. "When I looked at his face I was amazed at his peaceful expression and felt he was with the Lord. I prayed that I could find your phone number in order to give you this message."

The following story is an example of a transformation that occurred during a person's final moments. In some cases, evidence that the prodigal has changed only comes in the final days or moments of life.

Removing the Veil of Darkness

Louise and her husband were devastated when they learned their only son, Barry, had chosen to follow a homosexual lifestyle. Over and over they asked God to search their hearts to help them make sense of their disappointment. *Where could we have failed as parents?* they asked themselves. He had been raised in church and in a Christian home, with loving parents and grandparents.

In some cases, evidence that the prodigal has changed only comes in the final days or moments of life.

"We were grieved by the terrible choice Barry made," Louise said. "But at the time, none of us realized it would lead to his early death. After he took a job at a university in a distant state, we didn't see him often, but we kept in touch and let him know we loved him. We lamented the fact that Barry would never know the joys of parenthood, nor would we have his children as cherished grandchildren. But all we could do was pray for him."

The day came when Louise and her husband learned their son had developed AIDS. When they rushed to his side, he begged them to let him stay at his own apartment rather than go to a hospice. "We agreed," she said, "and then reorganized his apartment to become a hospital and rented an apartment across the hall for ourselves. I stayed there, and my husband and daughter commuted as often as they could to be with us. At one point we wondered whether God had given him up—but we kept praying and trusting God to intervene."

God's intervention came in the form of a friend's son. Jack came almost daily to visit Barry. The two young men had an instant rapport. "He took our son through the Scriptures over and over—lovingly sharing with him his need to come to full repentance in order to enjoy God's peace," Louise said. "Jack also enlisted many people to pray that he could get through to Barry."

One morning Barry told his parents of a dramatic vision he'd seen during the night. "I saw this big hand holding a large book," he said. "A loving voice said, 'Barry, this book is your life, and inside it are black pages. We are going to take these black pages out, one by one, and lay them on the table. I want you to confess to Me the sin of each black page.' "

"Mother, it's amazing!" he said. "I feel as if I'm already cleansed—is this deliverance? You'd better get Jack here. Now I understand the things you two have been saying to me for three months, and I see that my lifestyle is wrong. I've wasted so many years—can you ever forgive me?"

Louise told us it seemed God had supernaturally removed the veil of darkness from his eyes. "In the end, my son truly was born again," she said. "Though blind and almost totally paralyzed, at last he could see with spiritual eyes, and he had peace with God. During the final 10 days of his life, he told all his visitors—many from the gay community—about his wonderful transformation.

"Barry is home with the Lord, and he has no more pain. We miss him terribly, but home is where we're all going if we know Jesus. Because Barry surrendered his will to Jesus, God overwhelms us with hope for everlasting life together. His 33 years here are a short span compared to eternity. As time passes and I occasionally feel lonely for my only son, the Lord reminds me of the words He once spoke to a friend in New York whose son had been killed: 'I have your son, and you have Mine.' "[3]

It's Time to Get Serious

Single parenting is a hard enough job, even if the child develops no serious issues of rebellion. But when a child does become a prodigal, a single mom or dad often feels very much alone in coping with the situation. This was true in Marjorie's case. From the time her son, Justin, was five, she raised him in church and Christian schools. He accepted the Lord at an early age. But it seemed his whole life was a battle because of his father's negative influence on him. Justin attended one year at a Christian college but then strayed from the Lord at age 20.

"I did much spiritual warfare prayer for him," Marjorie said. "Sometimes I would walk by his shoes on the living room floor and be burdened to pray over them. I talked with him constantly, encouraging him to trust the Lord to help him with his struggles. Several years after he had turned away from God, I cried when he asked me for a devotional book. For his 25th birthday I bought him a book by Tony Evans called *It's Time to Get Serious*."

Just seven months after that, Justin was back in church, sitting beside her in the second row. For the next seven months they went to lunch together every Sunday.

"Over his favorite Mexican food, we talked about how he was struggling. I loved him unconditionally. He would say, 'I always disappoint you,' and I would reply, 'Justin, you will never disappoint me. Maybe some of your actions and behavior do, but not you.' I prayed, talked, listened—even preached some—but I kept the doors open."

After finishing the devotional book, Justin called his mom and asked for another one. But a few nights later, while driving home late from the restaurant where he worked, he fell asleep at the wheel and was killed in a head-on collision with a truck.

"When I got the news that he had been killed instantly, it seemed my whole world fell apart," Marjorie said. "I was unable to work for a year, but now God is slowly healing and restoring me. My only comfort is knowing that my returned prodigal is safe in our heavenly Father's arms."

The Calling of an Intercessor

Dixie and her husband are examples of parents who had to hear from God for themselves—and then go against the tide of advice they received from well-meaning Christian friends. Sometimes God asks us to make a decision in spite of disapproval or judgment from others. The road to obedience is not always easy.

What would you do if you learned that your son, who had AIDS, wanted to move home with his companion, who also was infected? Dixie and her husband prayed a long time before saying yes to these two moving into their nearby guest cottage. She writes:

It has been almost a dozen years since we became aware of our son's HIV status. At that time not much information was available on the disease. I stayed in disinterested denial—except to God. Mumbling and complaining was my comfort zone. I could vent and there was always agreement from my comforters. Disgust and disappointment became my own sin.

When we first found out about Mike's homosexual lifestyle, I wrote a prayer on a napkin while sitting in McDonald's: "Lord, I don't know how You can stand this. I thought I could but I just can't." I wrote several paragraphs, signed my name and sat there, waiting.

God's answer was swift: *Pray! I will show you mighty, inaccessible things that only I can reveal.*

On one occasion, knowing that He understood a mother's heart, I asked God: "Do you remember when Mike was a little baby? He was so tiny, precious and perfect. Oh, Father, I could love him then; why can't I love him like that now?"

Later, another day of frustration arrived. Self-absorbed and critical, I took a long walk and spoke to God again: "He acts like a little baby boy! Why doesn't he grow up?"

Clearly I heard the still, small voice of the Holy Spirit, *You said you could love him like a little baby. Can you?*

"I'll try, Lord."

Now I had not just one but two "children"—my son and Rodney, his partner. Rodney was near my age, well-educated and aloof. Aha! Finally I had someone to blame. I was so offended to see these two act like husband and wife. I complained to God.

I have called you to be an intercessor, He answered me.

One of my friends said, "You have entertained sin by allowing them to live on your property. Their sin will come upon you." Others cited examples from their own lives. I was torn and fearful. I could not offend God. Yet, weren't we to be merciful? Where would they go? Questions and emotions intermingled.

As my husband and I prayed further for guidance, God assured us that reaching out in mercy to Mike and Rodney was His plan for us. With this assurance we took the stand of faith in the midst of our friends' doctrinal opinions and harsh judgments.

I could not change these two men; therefore, it was I who began to change. The Holy Spirit and my husband were always there with unconditional love both for me and for Mike and Rodney.

Jesus Standing with Me

The disease, with its many symptoms and manifestations, was beginning to deteriorate Mike and Rodney's relationship. Dixie remembers that time:

Rodney had become more and more depressed, and our son, Mike, was lost in a haze from abusing prescription medications. Though our son would not let me pray or speak about God to him, he encouraged Rodney to come to the Bible study class I taught at our house on Thursdays.

Sitting there—the only man in the circle of ladies—he came to know and accept Jesus. One prayer was answered! The women talked to Rod, shared their feelings, read the Bible and prayed for him. He had never experienced such a showering of love. For the first time he was able to perceive women in light of the reality of Jesus. He read Scripture aloud to us, his eloquent diction and resonant voice touching every heart. God's anointing would hover over us. We were all amazed.

One Thursday Rod told me he was not coming to our Bible study class. "I have to work on the computer at the AIDS task force." Sighing, he took a deep breath and said, "I'm so depressed and lonely."

Our son was now hospitalized for his drug addiction and was not there to comfort him. Rodney's own mind, clouded with the dementia of the disease, was giving in to fear. We didn't see Rod all weekend, but I left messages on his answering machine. On Sunday, as my husband and I left for church, ominous concern churned in my stomach.

The service was wonderful. My thoughts were renewed by the message. As the pastor left the podium, he stopped, quickly turned back and spoke. His words startled me: "Today some of you will go home and find that the enemy has come to rob you. Don't let him."

I heard the still, small voice inside of me say, *He is dead.*

When we got home I called Rodney. No answer. I got in bed and pulled the covers over my head, feeling safe, while my husband went out to the cottage. Soon the phone rang. My husband had found Rod dead; he had taken his own life.

The next evening I was the speaker at a Christian women's meeting. I spoke of the love of Jesus. My body trembled and my heart ached. But in the midst of the confusion it seemed as though Jesus was there standing with me, unfailing and steadfast. I leaned on His presence and felt assurance that Rod truly was with Jesus, whom he had acknowledged as Savior. Others around me may have thought differently, but I sensed that Rod was finally home and whole.

"Furious winds often drive the vessel more swiftly into port," wrote British preacher Charles Haddon Spurgeon in the nineteenth century. How furious the winds? I'm still in awe to realize that the more we are buffeted by those winds, the more victorious we become.

We continue to trust God for Mike's salvation. At this writing we have no communication with him. He is in another relationship in a country halfway across the world—sick and nearer to death from his disease. But God has called me to an even deeper place of intercession, and I must trust Him![4]

Finally Home!

Barbara Johnson, the mother of four sons, lost one son in Vietnam, another in an auto accident and suffered years of estrangement from a third, who lived a gay lifestyle but who finally came home to his parents and to the Lord.

Her firstborn, Tim, had made a profession of faith, but she was concerned that he seemed so indifferent to spiritual things. Then one summer he went to Alaska with friends, hoping to find work and some adventure. Soon the young men ran out of money; they still didn't have jobs and were ready to head home. When they stopped for gas, the attendant began witnessing to them and then invited them for a meal. They ended up staying with him for several weeks and their host helped them find construction jobs. But more importantly, he got them involved with a local Christian fellowship where other believers loved and nurtured them.

When Tim and one of his friends were heading home, he phoned his mom, full of enthusiasm for what God was doing in his life. Just five hours after that phone call, their car was involved in a head-on collision. The truck, driven by a drunken driver, was on the wrong side of the road. Both boys were instantly killed.

Barbara shares in one of her books the feelings she experienced when she had to go to the morgue to identify her son's body:

Although I experienced deep grief over the loss of my oldest son, I thank the Lord that I was not overwhelmed by my sorrow. The Lord had imparted to me an inner assurance and joy in the knowledge that somehow He was going to use the testimony of Tim's changed life to reach others for Himself. I felt the grace of God wrapping around my heart. . . . It was as if I could look up and see Tim standing there, all bright and smiling at me, saying, "Don't cry, Mother. I am here with Jesus. I am finally Home!"[5]

Darkness Is as Light to You

Pastor Ron Mehl offers these words of encouragement to all who are still praying for a prodigal:

> When the darkness comes into our lives, when light seems to vanish and we begin to feel as though the sun will never again break the heaviness of our night, *that* is the time to "trust in the name of the Lord." That is the time to rely on our God and wait for Him. Those who scramble around trying to manufacture their own light and comfort, apart from God, will only find hurt and sorrow at the end of the trail.[6]

For the intercessor still looking for the breakthrough he or she has long prayed for, the time of waiting may seem like a dark tunnel with no light at the end. One mother shared this with us about her own struggle:

> At a time when I felt almost overwhelmed by darkness and hopelessness about my prodigal, the Lord ministered to me through Psalm 139:11,12: "If I say, 'Surely the darkness will hide me and the light become night around me,' even the darkness will not be dark to you; the night will shine like the day, for darkness is as light to you." This verse helped me realize that God is bigger than what seems like darkness to me. Then He spoke Isaiah 45:3 to me: "I will give you the treasures of darkness, riches stored in secret places, so that you may know that I am the LORD." I'm still waiting for a breakthrough, but in the times of darkness I've come to know

the Lord in a deeper way than ever before—and that really is a treasure.

Be assured that the Father who loves us with an everlasting love is aware of the ache we feel from being alienated from our prodigals. His timetable is so different from ours. But He is with us every moment in our time of waiting.

Prayer

Lord, I've loved, I've prayed, I've believed, I've trusted, I've waited for a breakthrough for my prodigal. Please watch over _____ wherever he (she) is. Thank You for Your promise that _____ can't escape from Your love and care. But Lord, somehow reassure me that he (she) is okay. As I wait for signs of repentance, help me to keep my hope fixed on You, no matter how long it takes. I love You, Lord. Amen.

Questions to Think About

1. Do I acknowledge that God wants my prodigal back even more than I do and that with Him there are no hopeless cases?
2. Can I steadfastly trust God's faithfulness, whether or not I see with my eyes, in this life, the answer I'm praying for?

Notes

1. Peter Lord, *Keeping the Doors Open* (Tarrytown, NY: Fleming H. Revell, 1992), pp. 72-75.
2. Ibid., pp. 76-78.
3. From *A Woman's Guide to Getting Through Tough Times*, © 1998 by Quin Sherrer and Ruthanne Garlock. Published by Servant Publications, Box 8617, Ann Arbor, Michigan, 48107, pp. 124-129. Used with permission.
4. From *Listen, God Is Speaking to You*, © 1999 by Quin Sherrer. Published by Servant Publications, Box 8617, Ann Arbor, Michigan, 48107, pp. 45-48. Used with permission.
5. Barbara Johnson, *Where Does a Mother Go to Resign?* (Minneapolis: Bethany House, 1979, 1994), pp. 50, 51.
6. Ron Mehl, *God Works the Night Shift* (Sisters, OR: Multnomah Publishers, 1994), p. 130.

CHAPTER NINE

The Elder-Brother Syndrome

The older brother stalked off in an angry sulk and refused to join in. His father came out and tried to talk to him, but he wouldn't listen. The son said, "Look how many years I've stayed here serving you, never giving you one moment of grief, but have you ever thrown a party for me and my friends? Then this son of yours who has thrown away your money on whores shows up and you go all out with a feast!"

—LUKE 15:28-30, *THE MESSAGE*

We have a self-righteous, overly responsible brother attempting to maintain his own sense of adequacy while trying to please his

father. He was so caught up in this that he failed to see his father's
gracious heart. He was so full of pride that it led to judgment. He
was angry, resentful, full of rules that he probably couldn't even
keep himself. He was sorry to see his brother return.[1]

—H. NORMAN WRIGHT

In a nutshell, the elder-brother syndrome is the tendency to judge everyone's sins and mistakes except our own. Jesus' account of the elder brother's response to the prodigal's return seems intended to expose the judgmental attitude of the Pharisees. To them, keeping the Law was more important than showing compassion to sinners. No doubt they were horrified by the father's actions in the parable—running to embrace a filthy runaway.

Jesus ended the story without giving the elder brother's response to his father's appeal to forgive his brother and rejoice in his return. The parable ends with an implied question for all who have received God's mercy: Since you have been forgiven, shouldn't you be willing to offer forgiveness?

Over and over throughout the New Testament we learn the necessity of forgiving those who have wronged us. James wrote, "For there will be no mercy to those who have shown no mercy. But if you have been merciful, then God's mercy toward you will win out over his judgment against you" (James 2:13, *TLB*). Just as we have freely received God's mercy when we didn't deserve it, we should extend mercy to others.

Pastor David Wilkerson says, "I believe it is the uncharitable Christian, so harsh and unforgiving, who drives the sinner away from the redeeming power of Christ. . . . Christians, who are themselves victims of all manner of temptations, often shut out the habituated by telling them they are hopeless cases."[2]

Are We Judging or Praying?

The younger brother was lost as he yielded to wanderlust for the far country. The older brother was lost to his arrogance and pride. How easy it is to feel smug, secure and self-righteous within the Church, while disdainfully regarding those outside as "the lost."

On one of my first visits to New York many years ago, I (Ruthanne) was with my husband and our host pastor, who was driving us around the city. While we were waiting at a traffic light, I looked out the car window and saw a man who had stepped into a glass-walled phone booth to escape the cold wind. He was drunk and had passed out, but the restricted space in the phone booth caused him to sort of crumple into a heap.

How could a person allow himself to stoop so low and get into such a condition? was the self-righteous thought going through my mind.

But God knew my heart and read my thoughts. And instantly I heard His response: *Why are you criticizing him? My Son died for him, just as He died for you. You should be praying for him instead of condemning him.*

This entire exchange took place in only a few seconds, but it left a lasting impression. I repented for my spiritual pride and asked the Lord's forgiveness and then prayed that God would send someone across that man's path who could give him the Good News. Since then I've asked the Lord to help me see people at every level of society as He sees them and to help me have the compassion to pray for them, not to judge them.

Do We Love the Sinner?

Manny was a student at the Bible school where my husband, John, was teaching. He felt his ministry call was to the lowly and unlovely, the homeless street people, the ones who hardly provide the economic or social core of a thriving church. Even while still in school he spent weekends sharing food and witnessing to folks who lived under the bridges and overpasses in the more disreputable parts of Dallas. After graduating, he plunged full-time into reaching out to these people, scraping by on the meager support he received from a few who shared his heart for this task.

One Monday he phoned John with a sort of subdued anger in his voice. "Mr. Garlock," he said, "church so-and-so has helped me from time to time with special offerings. When I asked if they would be willing to accept some of my converts into the congregation, they always said yes. Well, Saturday night a couple of prostitutes and a pimp accepted Jesus on a street corner. I invited them to go to church with me on Sunday, but thought I should let the pastor know they'd be coming. Know what he said? He told me to take them to the Salvation Army or one of the skid-row missions. 'My people aren't ready to have folks like that among us,' he told me. Sometimes it's hard not to get mad at such Christians . . ."

Manny later told John he has several open doors for presenting his work, showing a video and making an appeal. One church even bought him a new van to use for food distribution.

But the attitude seemed to be, "You go ahead and do the work, Manny. We'll give you the money so we won't have to."

A young woman who once demonstrated for abortion rights came to Christ. She gives a sad commentary on how she was treated by many Christians. "Too often, the words and actions of Christians pushed me farther away from Jesus," she said. "Christians need to stop using Saint Augustine's line, 'love the sinner, hate the sin.' As a lesbian feminist activist, I felt despised, judged, and condemned by Christians. It seemed that they had the 'hate' part down, but their 'love' of me never went any deeper than words."[3]

Perhaps each of us should ask ourselves, *Is my attitude like the father's in the Luke 15 passage—ready to receive a detestable prodigal with open arms? Or would I respond with disdain as the elder brother did?*

Letting Go of Comparisons

Author Henri Nouwen takes a penetrating look at this issue:

Often we think about lostness in terms of actions that are quite visible, even spectacular. The younger son sinned in a way we can easily identify. His lostness is quite obvious. He misused his money, his time, his friends, his own body. What he did was wrong; not only his family and friends knew it, but he himself as well. . . .

The lostness of the elder son, however, is much harder to identify. After all, he did all the right things. He was obedient, dutiful, law-abiding, and hardworking. . . .

Outwardly, the elder son was faultless. But when confronted by his father's joy at the return of his younger brother, a dark power erupts in him and boils to the surface. Suddenly, there becomes glaringly visible a resentful, proud, unkind, selfish person, one that had remained deeply hidden. . . .

The father does not compare the two sons. He loves them both with a complete love and expresses that love according to their individual journeys. . . .

I have to let go of all comparison, all rivalry and competition, and surrender to the Father's love. This requires a leap of faith because I have little experience of non-comparing love and do not know the healing power of such a love. As long as I stay outside in the darkness, I can only remain in the resentful complaint that results from my comparisons. Outside of the light, my younger brother seems to be more loved by the Father than I; in fact, outside of the light, I cannot even see him as my own brother.[4]

You Are the Older Brother

One woman wrote to share how the Lord dealt with her about her elder-brother attitude:

Growing up in an abusive home, I continually tried to do what my father wanted so I could please him and avoid the pain of his wrath. That set me up for the abuse to become sexual. I felt trapped. Each time I wanted to matter to someone, I would seek to do what that person liked to win favor. I married David and things didn't change.

Then five years ago we both came to the Lord and began our walk with Him. I became very involved in church with teaching beginners, cleaning and helping wherever someone needed help. In Bible studies I learned about what God wants of us, but over time I became drained and worn out. I could feel God talk to me, but I reached a point where I just couldn't hear what He was saying. This went on and on.

My sister found the Lord about the same time I did, but her walk was so different. In my eyes I would see her going away from God. Then when things got real bad for her, she'd run back to Him and God would bless her. Then after a time she'd go back to the old way and when things went real bad again, she'd run back to God and He would bless her. This made me angry. Not that God wasn't blessing me—I felt blessed all the time. I was angry because it seemed I was working to get close to God and she was being flaky.

Then a guest speaker came to our church and preached on the prodigal son. But he focused on the older brother. I always had read the story with the thought, *Oh, that's good for those who are lost*—not giving a thought to the older brother. I realized that I related to the older brother's resentment. In my heart I had deep hurts and fears.

The next day at a women's Bible study, I asked for prayer. As I was worshiping God and thanking Him with tears streaming down my face, I felt God say to me, *You are the older brother!* I cried harder. I said, "No, God, I love you." He replied, *Yes. Don't you know you have always been with me and everything I have is yours? I have been with you always.*

Suddenly a parade of events in my life played out across my mind. I realized I was coming to Him out of a sense of duty and a fear of rejection—the same attitude I'd had toward my earthly father. Yet each time, God extended His covering, mercy, grace and love. He showed me I can do nothing to earn His love.

I'm beginning to understand that I must allow the Holy Spirit to draw me, and then I must be obedient to follow. Long ago I repented for my older-brother attitude and have watched God take it away and replace it with joy that I'm one of His children!

Sibling Rivalry Crushes Joy

The elder brother's resentment of the younger upon his return reveals a sour relationship which may have been part of the reason the prodigal left home in the first place. The father willingly received the wanderer back into the household as his son and longed to see his firstborn accept him back as his brother. But pride and stubbornness made the elder brother completely intolerant. Had he been willing to forgive his errant brother, the father's joy in the celebration would have been truly complete.

Dr. H. Norman Wright says:

The younger [brother] . . . came home after spending all of his inheritance, which was no small amount. It wasn't anything he had earned, yet his father pulled out all the stops: new clothes, new jewelry, the best calf for a barbecue and a party. There is nothing said of punishment, lectures, restrictions or earning of trust. . . .

My guess is that [the elder brother] was not as incensed by his younger brother's return or his father's forgiveness of him as he was by the celebration.[5]

"I remember the hurt we felt when our son's siblings treated him this way," one mother told us. "We were thrilled that our son came home for a holiday gathering with the entire family, but the resentment his brother and sister showed toward him almost ruined the occasion. We had prayed for weeks that he would agree to come home for this event. And of course we knew our prodigal was not squeaky clean, but we felt that receiving him with love would influence him in the best possible way. Instead, we struggled over our frustration with the older kids, while trying to keep everything on an even keel with strained relationships. It made me appreciate the disappointment the father of the prodigal must have felt."

A Gracious God

Jonah, the Old Testament prophet commissioned to go preach repentance in the city of Nineveh, is a classic example of one who had an elder-brother mentality. Instead of obeying God, he boarded a ship going the opposite direction from Nineveh. When a violent storm hit, his shipmates threw him into the sea and he ended up in the belly of a great fish. From there he prayed and cried out for help.

God delivered him, and Jonah obeyed by going to Nineveh. His message—that God would destroy them if they didn't repent—had a dramatic impact. The entire city, from the king on down, repented and turned from their evil ways, and God relented from destroying the city.

But Jonah resented this show of mercy. He complained to God, "This is exactly what I thought you'd do, Lord, when I was there in my own country and you first told me to come here. That's why I ran away to Tarshish. For I knew you were a gracious God, merciful, slow to get angry, and full of kindness; I knew how easily you could cancel your plans for destroying these people" (Jon. 4:1,2, *TLB*).

The book of Jonah ends with God's question: "And why shouldn't I feel sorry for a great city like Nineveh with its 120,000 people in utter spiritual darkness?" (Jon. 4:11, *TLB*).

Obviously God's attitude toward those who repent is the same as the father's toward the prodigal. The parable ends with the father's words: "But it is right to celebrate. For he is your brother; and he was dead and has come back to life! He was lost and is found!" (Luke 15:31, *TLB*).

God, How Could You?

Vickie's haughty attitude about a repentant brother was not a lot different from Jonah's. Late one night when she sleepily answered the phone, she heard her brother shout, "Sis, I just invited Jesus into my life! I'm saved. The preacher said to tell someone immediately, so I had to call you. I imagine you've prayed for me for a long time."

His sister sat speechless with the phone in her hand. *God, how could You?* she asked with a self-righteous attitude. Then she reminded God, *This brother of mine—the one who mocked and screamed at me at our mother's funeral when I tried to talk to him about Mom's receiving the Lord before she died—this man who broke up a pastor's home to marry his third and current wife, has actually accepted Christ? This rebel is now a Christian? I can hardly believe it.*

Why is it when our loved ones are rescued in answer to our prayers, we tend to be surprised? Still in shock, Vickie called me (Quin) the morning after her brother's announcement. "That's wonderful—don't you remember the many times we prayed together for him?" I said. I rejoiced while she took time to get rid of her elder-brother attitude.

Why is it when our loved ones are rescued in answer to our prayers we tend to be surprised?

When I saw Vickie's brother at her daughter's wedding, I could tell there had truly been a change in him.

No One Deserves Grace

Philip Yancey says, "Grace comes free of charge to people who do not deserve it and I am one of those people. I think back to who I was—resentful, wound tight with anger, a single hardened link in a long chain of ungrace learned from family and church. Now I am trying in my own small way to pipe the tune of grace. . . . I yearn for the church to become a nourishing culture of that grace.[6]

After spending a weekend in Washington, DC, to observe a Gay Pride march, Philip Yancey wrote of the experience:

Every person I interviewed could tell hair-raising tales of rejection, hatred, and persecutions. Most had been called names and beaten up too many times to count. Half of the people I interviewed had been disowned by their families. Some of the AIDS patients had tried to contact their estranged families to inform them of the disease but had received no response. One man, after ten years of separation, was invited home for Thanksgiving dinner. His mother seated him apart from the family, at a separate table set with Chinette plates and plastic utensils.

Some Christians say, "Yes, we should treat gays with compassion but at the same time we must give them a message of judgment." After all these interviews, I began to understand that every gay person has [already] heard the message of judgment from the church—again and again.[7]

Letting Go of Judgment

Edith and Bob are parents who tried the best way they knew to instill Christian values in their children. But in dealing with Penny, their prodigal daughter, the Lord showed them the prejudice in their own hearts.

Penny had just graduated with honors from high school and was about to leave for a Christian college. She'd been working at a fast-food restaurant and partying with her friends after work. One summer day she packed up and left, leaving her folks a surprise Dear Parents letter saying she wanted a vacation from home. She asked them not to try to find her but to forgive and pray for her.

"Looking back, we were really too strict, too protective," Edith said. "Both Bob and I had been wild before we became Christians, and we wanted to make sure Penny and our sons didn't follow suit. But our holding the reins too tightly only caused her to rebel against us.

"At first we didn't know where she was. Later we found out she had a different job and had moved in with her boss, Matt, who was divorced and had two children. This was especially hard for Bob—he seemed to feel divorce was an unforgivable sin. I was afraid if we showed love to her, she'd think we approved of this relationship. Even our pastor counseled us to no longer have anything to do with her—this was in the days when you didn't hear much about unmarried couples living together. We visited a pastor in another state and he encouraged us *not* to cast her aside, saying we might be the only light in her life right now. To us that seemed right and more like what Jesus would do."

Edith went to a motel alone for a weekend to fast and pray for her daughter, as she and Bob had done many times before. This time, when she opened the Bible to Jeremiah 31:16,17 it became her lifeline: " 'Restrain your voice from weeping and your eyes from tears, for your work will be rewarded,' declares the LORD. 'They will return from the land of the enemy. So there is hope for your future,' declares the LORD. 'Your children will return to their own land.' "

Edith stopped crying and started believing that her daughter would come back. Five years later, Penny did return. Today she and Matt are married and have a beautiful Christian family.

Recently, I (Quin) asked Edith what, in addition to prayer, was the key that brought about the change.

"I would say we dealt with our own prejudices and legalistic views. It was as if God was waiting for Bob to see that divorce is not the unpardonable sin and to forgive and release this fellow. Once my husband let go of judgment and forgave Matt, he and Penny married. We both had to rest in God. Finally, I concluded that if God could patiently wait on her return, then so could I. After all, He loves her far more than I ever could. So I decided to quit striving and just trust Him."

Not long ago I had lunch with all four of them, and you couldn't find a happier Christian foursome. God truly has done a work of restoration in this family.

A Pharisee's Attitude

Sometimes we parents forget what we were like before Jesus rescued us—not unlike the self-righteous Pharisees Jesus warned against. Parents who once were into drugs or alcohol want to spare their children the heartache and emptiness they experienced. So they may lecture, preach, threaten or react with a judgmental attitude.

Our children probably need to know about our own weaknesses or addictions that once held us captive. As God grants us the humility to be honest with them, we can share at an appropriate time some of our past mistakes and how God had mercy on us. Without this humble transparency we can become overly judgmental and condemning; harsh legalism usually proves to be counterproductive.

I (Quin) am one who believes in harvesting the best in each generation. The Bible records many mistakes—David's adultery with Bathsheba, Abraham's Ishmael, Joseph's brothers' betrayal,

Paul's persecution of Christians—yet we have the record of God's mercy extended to each of these people.

On the other hand, as parents we cannot live on the dead-end street of "if only," for it goes nowhere. "If only I'd been more strict, less strict, moved him to another school, forbade him to associate with those friends, taken away his car privileges . . . ," and so it goes. Guilt overwhelms. But we can ask God, as well as our children, to forgive us for the ways we were negligent, irresponsible or too harsh. Then we must leave that guilt at the Cross and receive His forgiveness.

Unconditional love—such as the father in the parable offered to his younger son—is the thing every returning prodigal yearns for. Margie Lewis reminds us how important this is:

> Unconditional love is not always an overwhelming, uncontrollable feeling. It is more than just an emotion or a heartfelt warmth. Unconditional love is a conscious choice. And sometimes, when the feelings sag, it may be mostly resolve. It is as much a matter of the mind and will as of the heart. . . .
>
> Kind acts take real effort and determination in the face of our hurts and concerns, but they are essential. Our expressions and claims of love ring hollow without kindness.[8]

We always love our children. We may not love their behavior, dress or friends, but we love them as people—God's gift to us. And even when they are adults making decisions we don't agree with, still we love them. Why? Because that's the way God loves us.

When the prodigals begin coming home, let's welcome, embrace and restore them with God's love.

Prayer

Lord, forgive me for my self-righteous judging of others—forgetting to examine my own sin, forgetting even how far I was from You. But You accepted me just as I was, and I'm no better than any other sinner. Please don't let my wrong attitudes turn off a prodigal needing to find his (her) way back to You. Lord, I give You permission to deal with me so my heart and arms are ready to receive any prodigal—mine or another's. Check me when I need to reexamine my reactions. Help me to love with Your love and to be an instrument of reconciliation. Amen.

Questions to Think About

1. In what ways have I exhibited the elder brother attitude toward my prodigal?
2. Do I show this attitude toward prodigals who visit my church or live in my community or are a part of my workplace?

Notes

1. H. Norman Wright, *Sisters and Brothers Forever* (Ventura, CA: Regal Books, 1999), p. 34.

2. David Wilkerson, *Two of Me* (Lindale, TX: Garden Valley Publishers, 1980), pp. 15, 16.

3. Frederica Mathewes-Green, "Chasing Amy," *Christianity Today* (January 10, 2000), p. 60.

4. Henri J. M. Nouwen, *The Return of the Prodigal Son* (New York: Doubleday, Image Books, 1992), pp. 70, 71, 80, 81.

5. Wright, *Sisters and Brothers Forever,* pp. 33, 34.

6. Taken from *What's So Amazing About Grace?* by Philip Yancey. Copyright © 1997 by Philip D. Yancey. Used by permission of Zondervan Publishing House, p. 37.

7. Ibid., p. 151.

8. Margie M. Lewis, *The Hurting Parent* (Grand Rapids, MI: Zondervan Publishing House, 1980), pp. 81, 83.

CHAPTER TEN

Encouragement for Those Who Wait

Encourage the exhausted, and strengthen the feeble. Say to those with anxious heart, "Take courage, fear not. Behold, your God will come with vengeance; the recompense of God will come, but He will save you."

—ISAIAH 35:3,4, *NASB*

There is no escape from the God who is everywhere. He is there and He is ceaselessly calling His own back to the Father's house.[1]

—TOM BISSET

I f you are in a holding pattern, praying and waiting expectantly for a prodigal, take heart! God has not forgotten you. "Authentic hope is always a by-product of a personal relationship with God," says Pastor Lloyd Ogilvie, "a vibrant expectation of His timely interventions in keeping with His gracious promises to us."[2]

Our friend Barbara Johnson is the founder of an outreach called Spatula Ministries. It exists to encourage and uplift parents whose children have become prodigals—especially if those sons or daughters have embraced a gay lifestyle. She sees herself as helping to scrape traumatized parents off the ceiling—hence the name of the ministry.

Barbara has received thousands of letters from the people whose lives she has touched, and she often shares them in her Spatula newsletter. Following are excerpts from two parents' letters whose prodigals are in gay relationships:

> Given time, the wounds will heal and they will be able to smile and laugh again. The parents' only job right now is to love their child. They do not have to understand, they do not have to try to change their child (only God can do that anyway). They just need to love, love, love their child. The reason I can say this is that I speak from experience. . . . I still do not approve of my daughter's lifestyle, but I praise God for the good relationship we have with her.

> We now choose to put our son in the hands of God. We can love him unconditionally and pray for him. Our son has since told us that the finest gift we ever gave him was when he knew his dad could and would still love him

and call him his son, and that he really was still a part of
our family. . . . Unconditional love is not easy. It takes
time, it takes soul-searching and a direct prayer line with
God.

And from a prodigal daughter who returned:

I want to encourage parents who feel pain and disappointment caused by their wayward child to PRAY,
PRAY, PRAY, and PRAY SOME MORE! I am one of
those wayward children, but I've made my way to the
Lord. Both my parents are mighty prayer warriors. I
know without a doubt that it was their prayers that
brought me to my knees ready to repent.

I was an alcoholic, a smoker, did drugs, was very sexually active starting at the age of 16 and thought I knew
everything. I got involved with the wrong kind of
friends. I was very mean and manipulative. One day, as
my father stood picketing an abortion clinic, I put my
nose in the air and killed their grandchild.

Did they forgive me? With God's grace, yes they did!
Through Christian counseling and many tears we've
restored our relationship.

I know there were days when my parents felt their
prayers were not being heard, let alone answered, but
they kept praying and trusting Christ. In His perfect
timing, I made my commitment to Christ and the uphill
climb to restoration and healing. There will be days
when the dark tunnel will go on and on for miles, but
just remember there is light at the end of it—God's
light![3]

God's Restoration

One mother who continues to pray for her prodigal has found a lifeline of hope in this Scripture: "I have seen his ways, but I will heal him; I will guide him and restore comfort to him, creating praise on the lips of the mourners" (Isa. 57:18,19).

She said, "One morning in prayer the Lord spoke to me very clearly through these verses that my son would be healed of his wandering. A few years earlier I had heard an anointed soloist sing about the woman at the well. One line said, 'I will never, never thirst again. . . .' I asked God to give that living water to my son, and He spoke this word of assurance: *I know exactly where he is every moment; My eye is continually upon him.* When the Holy Spirit drew my attention to this passage in Isaiah, I remembered what God had spoken earlier and received it as His promise that my son will be restored."

Tom Bisset writes in his excellent book *Why Christian Kids Leave the Faith*:

> It does not matter that these wanderers refuse to listen or that they will not attend church or that they become silent when the conversation turns to spiritual things. It does not even matter if they refuse to read the Bible or to pray. What matters is that they cannot escape from the God who is everywhere and who is always speaking.[4]

Searching for Acceptance

Diane and her husband faced a great challenge with Michael, their high-energy, musically gifted son who sometimes was quite rebellious. But Michael did know the Lord, and his parents hung on to an assurance that this son would fulfill the destiny God had planned for him. After he had gone away to college, Michael called home one day with shocking news: "Mom, Dad, I think you are wasting your money to send me to college. I want to come home and do music."

"In today's vernacular that meant he wanted to join a band, write music and hopefully get paid for it," Diane said. "He did come home. He joined several bands, wrote music and did get paid for his work. His life took a different turn from what most Christian parents expect, but we supported him in his decisions. We kept our faith in what we felt God had promised: 'when he is old he will not depart from it' (Prov. 22:6, *NASB*).

Be tenacious in your faith that God will use your children's talents and gifts to bring glory to Him, regardless of your own timetable or expectations.

"When Michael played in nightclubs or bars, we went to see him and clapped the loudest. When he wanted approval for the latest line he'd written or sound he'd created, we gave it. His dad spent many hours, as an audience of one, supporting Michael's music dreams.

"A few years ago Michael's aunt prophesied that she saw him as a praise and worship leader in the church. He wasn't quite ready to hear that at the time but accepted it nevertheless. Today Michael is a successful businessman with a beautiful wife and two children. And he is a worship leader at church and plays guitar at Christian conferences around the country. This is not just the story of a prodigal who returned, but of parents who never stopped believing that what

ENCOURAGEMENT FOR THOSE WHO WAIT 181

was in their son's heart was alive and real and would come to fruition."

Don't give up. Be tenacious in your faith that God will use your children's talents and gifts to bring glory to Him, regardless of your own timetable or expectations.

A Hunger for Love

Most prodigals try to fill their need for love with the wrong choices the devil brings across their paths. Chuck's story aptly illustrates this scenario. This young man grew up in a Christian home, the son of missionaries to Central America. Yet for years he secretly struggled with the lure of same-sex attractions and the guilt he felt when he yielded to those temptations. Chuck writes of his journey to wholeness:

My early childhood memories involve mostly my mom and my older sister, who was my primary playmate. Dad, a workaholic, seemed to be gone most of the time. He became a Christian when I was five and then felt God was leading him to become a missionary. Over the next five years we lived in three different states while Dad attended seminary and language school.

I always felt different from other boys. As a nine-year-old white kid living in a Texas border town, I was in the minority. Gangs of boys often harassed me as I walked to and from school. After we moved to Central America I struggled to make friends because I knew only a few words of Spanish. Dad's itinerant ministry meant we traveled from church to church, so I never felt as if I really belonged anywhere. Sometimes I'd watch a group of boys playing soccer and wish I was athletic like them and surrounded by friends. Then one day I innocently and accidentally discovered masturbation. It became a regular way to numb my loneliness.

Since Dad followed the example of the workaholic missionaries who were his role models, I didn't get to see him often. But he really didn't know how to connect with me anyway or how to provide the affirmation I craved from him. I had a hole in my soul that needed to be filled by a man's love. When legitimate relationships didn't develop to fill the need, I became vulnerable for an illegitimate one.

One day as I walked alone through a shopping plaza after attending an action thriller movie, a young man in his late 20s approached me. Strangers often would try to converse with me to practice their English, so I thought nothing of it. This handsome man with a winning smile appeared genuinely interested in me. His dark eyes seemed to look right into me as we talked. When he offered me a ride home, at first I hesitated, but finally I agreed because he just seemed so nice. Little did I realize that accepting a ride home with a stranger would stamp that day on my soul for years to come.

As he drove he reached over to hold my hand. But his hand didn't stop there. He had taken the scenic route home and now pulled over in an out-of-the-way place. I thought my heart would pound out of my chest. Feeling paralyzed, I just let him do what he wanted. By the time I arrived home I had experienced my first sexual encounter. It was both wonderful and dreadful. I loved the attention from a man, but I felt guilty, afraid and confused.

Now my fantasy had a focus. I began to feel even more different from others, and my male identity eroded away. I truly loved Jesus and wanted to please Him, but brewing deep inside me was a dark storm. I compartmentalized my life and allowed others in only to a certain point. Down deep I knew my fantasy was sin. But the scream of my hunger for love, combined with my awakened libido, was so intense it drowned out the voice of the Holy Spirit.

I Couldn't Handle Problems Alone

After high school graduation, Chuck returned to the States, resolving to put the past behind him to follow the path of Bible college, marriage and missions—a son his dad would be proud of. He did okay for awhile, but to his dismay his attraction to men did not go away—it intensified. He was lonely, far away from his family and in a new culture. His letter continues a story of confusion and despair:

I was too terrified to talk to anyone, but I couldn't handle these problems alone either.

When my scholarship ran out, I moved off campus and got a secular job—isolating me from other Christians. It was only a matter of time before I was having occasional sexual encounters. Feeling guilty and depressed, I would cry out to God and promise never to do it again—only to fall again. This cycle imprinted an identity of failure on my soul.

A customer at work who was openly gay befriended me and became my first real relationship. I liked not feeling that I had to hide something from him. One day he talked me into going to one of the gay bars in town. Before long I knew them all— including the drag shows and the drinking. The protective walls of innocence around my heart came down one by one, and I couldn't see that Satan was raising his strongholds in their place.

Although I tried to keep up appearances, I eventually was found out and my pastor came knocking on my door. Of course I wanted to go straight. (As one partner put it, "Who wouldn't give their right arm to go straight?") So I submitted to everything I was asked to do, including going to a man who was supposed to minister deliverance to me. He offered no in-depth counseling—just a few questions to determine if I wanted to change, and I said yes. But no accountability was set up and I was still confused. All my false belief systems were still in place. On the way home, as I passed a gay bar, I instinctively turned in.

I received ministry more than once. Each time, I fell but couldn't bring myself to talk to anyone. Shame, fear and rejection controlled me. I didn't know how to fight the magnetic power that kept pulling me into bars and dark encounters. After a few false starts at getting free, I was even more depressed and felt I was a total failure.

But thank God, the Holy Spirit kept working on my case. I may have felt out of place and miserable in church, but I was even more miserable away from God. I decided to make a fresh start and moved to a small southwestern town. There, I lived almost totally free from encounters with other men, but only because of lack of opportunity. I hid in a Christian environment and worked full-time with a group of missionaries.

After a few years I thought I was doing well enough to go back East to finish Bible college and follow in my father's footsteps. I was really seeking Dad's approval, but always felt sabotaged in my attempts to earn it. I didn't realize that my heavenly Father totally accepted and loved me apart from my performance.

Returning to the same work situation as before, I succumbed to the same temptations. I dropped out of school and

my days became a cycle of going to work and then either to the
gay bar or to my apartment where I would drink until I passed
out. Depressed and void of self-esteem, I had come to the end of
myself.

Finding the Answer

When his dad came to visit, Chuck tried to put on as good a
show as he could for him. He even went with his dad to a church
in another city where he was to minister. What a surprise when
the pastors invited Chuck to come and live there!

Meanwhile, a man in the town where he had been living was
courting him and wanted Chuck to move in with him. But
Chuck knew what he had to do. He continues:

Somewhere, somehow, surely God had an answer for me. I knew
I would not be at peace until I found it. Despite the man's plead-
ing to come live with him, I moved to make a new start and follow God.

I worked as a live-in aide to a retired gentleman who was
recovering from surgery. He and his wife were strong Christians
who helped bring stability and focus back into my life. They
made me feel genuinely welcomed and loved and treated me
with respect and kindness. It was a safe haven for me. He challenged me to memorize Scriptures, and as I did, my spiritual
man began to grow and receive strength.

One day an ex-gay minister came to our church for a series
of meetings. Curious to know whether he was for real or not, I
went to a reception I knew he would be attending. When I

approached and got close to him, it felt as if someone suddenly plunged a claw deep into my belly and twisted it. If I had doubted before that I was demonized, all doubt left at that moment. I believe the evil spirit recognized the authority this minister had and was afraid.

I made an appointment to see him, but he would not minister deliverance to me right away. First, he insisted I listen to some of his teaching. This man's focus is on our identity with Christ and renewing the mind with Scripture. At the end of that week I went to my ministry appointment, but I already felt free. This time I knew something had changed within me! In my pastor's home that day I truly was set free. I felt totally cleansed and light inside. I was filled with a joy I hadn't felt in years—I was on a spiritual high!

Just a few months later I met Doris, a beautiful, intelligent special-education teacher who attended our church. After four months of prayer and seeking God, we became engaged and were married a short time later. The small church was packed with people, but only a few knew what this day meant for Doris and me. Mom and Dad drove hundreds of miles to be there. They were so proud I was getting married.

Looking back, the only way it worked is that we were convinced God was directing us. Now, after more than 10 years, we are still convinced, still together and still best friends. Both of us needed lots of healing. But God met Doris and me where we were and used each of us to minister healing to the other. Our commitment to God's plan and to one another is the glue that has kept us together through thick and thin.

I still had emotional issues to overcome and wrong patterns of thinking to correct. I learned that regardless of orientation, sexual temptation is still just sexual temptation. Just because I was tempted didn't mean I had to sin. I also learned that a spiritual transaction had taken place when I was seduced as a young teen. And I recognized that my emotional needs for love from my father and legitimate male relationships were distorted and sexualized. Gaining new understanding of the events in my life provided another measure of freedom.

Though Doris and I have been through rough times, God has given us the grace to stay close. I thank God for our four great children. As I express my love to them, Father God reveals His love to me. Now, as a full-time minister, I find that gay or straight, most men are struggling with the same root problems—searching for love, identity and significance. I can tell them with confidence that Jesus Christ is the answer. What the devil meant for my destruction, I now use against him to help others. God is a God of hope and restoration, and what He has done for me He will do for anyone who seeks the help he needs.

With God, Nobody's Hopeless

Evangelist Billy Graham and his wife, Ruth, depended on God's faithfulness through the years they prayed for their rebellious son. In the afterword of Franklin Graham's book *Rebel With a Cause*, they wrote:

> We understood how difficult it must have been to have a well-known dad, yet we knew the rebellion was not against us personally. . . . In short, Franklin didn't have a chance. He had been given to God before his birth, and God has kept His hand on him without letting up all these years. . . .

When folks say, "You must be proud of Franklin," we realize that it is not a matter of pride, but of gratitude to God for His faithfulness.

With God, nobody's hopeless.[5]

Through years of disappointment, Renée's parents fought to hold on to their belief that with God, nobody is hopeless. At age 15, Renée became rebellious—opposing her parents' rules and authority and the Christian values they had instilled in her. She was attracted to the dark side of life and gradually began drinking and hanging out with a different group of friends. Once, when her parents were out of town, she was found drunk in a snowbank and rushed to a hospital where they pumped her stomach to spare her life. Her mother picks up the story:

The crushing blow came when Renée wanted an abortion. As a Christian family, this was most distressing. We would not sign for her, so she went out of state to get an abortion. You cannot imagine the pain all of this was to me. In order to preserve our reputation, we didn't feel we could share this information with anybody but the Lord. Our marriage was suffering. But we pressed in to the Lord and asked for godly wisdom to be responsible parents.

We learned that the antidote for depression is a thankful heart. Psalm 3:3 (*NASB*) became the living Word to me: "But Thou, O LORD, art a shield about me, my glory, and the One who lifts my head." We would personalize Scripture and substitute our daughter's name as we prayed, reminding the Lord of His promise.

For a few more years our daughter was an alcoholic, in and out of colleges, jobs and relationships with men. She ran off to another state and got into a relationship with a man who became abusive. Finding herself pregnant again, she decided it would be best to marry. However, at this point she came to her senses just as the prodigal son did in the Bible. She got back in touch with us and even listened to our counsel in a phone conversation.

"Two wrongs don't make a right," we told her. She said she feared for her life and wanted to leave, so we prayed that God would make a way of escape. She was able to drive to a safe place and finally to our home. Once here she made peace with God and with us. We gladly welcomed her back to the fold.

During the pregnancy, Renée realized how sacred life really is, and she began to follow the ways of the Lord. She and her son lived with us for five years while Renée started college again, finally graduating with honors and an elementary education degree. Today she is a creative, hard-working schoolteacher and a godly mother to her 10-year-old son. Truly, God was a shield about her, the glory and the One who lifts her head.

God's Limitless Mercy and Power

Valerie's daughter, Amy, became involved in lesbianism when she went away to college, launching her parents into a years-long prayer battle. At last Amy has returned from the far country, reconciled with her parents and is rebuilding her relationship with God. Valerie shares some of the lessons she's learned about children who get sucked into the gay lifestyle:

In my experience, about the only ones who come out of this lifestyle are those who were raised in genuine Christian homes and truly were born again. They don't want to spend eternity without their families. They do know in varying degrees what they are missing. Amy said that other gays saw there was a difference in her even when she was in the pit. She now recognizes the enemy's lies and deceptions to which she fell prey.

Bondage to this lifestyle has to run a much longer course of pain and disillusionment than parents can conceive. Amy suffered a lot physically and emotionally, hitting the bottom several times before she made the break. Interceding parents should pray every day that their prodigal's lifestyle will go sour and that the child will receive no satisfaction from it. Staying in it has to become much more painful than the pain of leaving it. At some point Amy began to realize that home was safer, warmer and happier than "out there." Home was something she did not want to lose. She began to understand how much we loved her and she loved us.

Pride is a luxury parents can't afford when wooing their child back from the pit. God gives grace to the humble! I never turned down an opportunity to receive prayer, and at many stages I had to repent of my own pride and wrong attitude.

God and His ways must come first in all decisions. Many times we had to choose between obeying God or doing what Amy wanted us to do. This may sound simple, but it isn't. It was the most difficult, soul-wrenching time of our lives. But we (including Amy) are much more aware of our weaknesses and, more importantly, of God's limitless mercy and power.

Your Tears Aren't Wasted

If you have grown a bit battle weary while praying for your prodigal, you may want to try what I (Quin) did to build my faith in time of discouragement over my children. I read biographies of great men and women of faith, looking for examples of how their moms had prayed.

Monica, the mother of Saint Augustine, is one of my favorites. At age 16, the rebellious young Augustine lived with a mistress, fathered an illegitimate son and eventually joined a heretical group, or cult.

In his *Confessions* he tells how God "drew his soul out of the profound darkness" because of his mother who, he says, wept on his behalf more than most mothers weep when their children die. When Monica asked a bishop to speak to her son, he refused, saying, "Leave him alone for a time . . . only pray to God for him. . . . Go thy way, and God bless thee, for it is not possible that the son of these tears should perish."[6]

It was Monica's persistent prayer for almost 19 years that brought her son to God. He later became one of the leading bishops of the Church in the fourth century.

As most parents of prodigals can testify, tears often accompany our prayers for a child who strays. In fact, sometimes weeping is the only type of prayer we can manage. Wesley Duewel assures us:

To pray with tears is to make an eternal investment. To pray with tears is to sow your tears with eternal harvest. No tear shed in burdened intercession for others is ever forgotten by God, unrecorded, or in vain. Intercession watered with tears is one of the most powerful forms of prayer known. As surely as God is in heaven, "Those who sow in tears will reap with songs of joy. He who goes out weeping, carrying seed to sow, will return with songs of joy, carrying sheaves with him" (Ps. 126:5,6).[7]

Hoping for Good News

Rhonda was the only one of Nancy's three who was a problem child. Though she never got in trouble with the law, she rebelled against her parent's rules and generally kept things in an uproar. Once, when she was 16, she ran away from home with a girlfriend. For three sleepless nights Nancy and her husband hoped and prayed for good news and for the girls' safekeeping.

When the girls came home, Nancy learned they had been in a nearby city, sleeping in their car at night just two blocks from where a notorious murderer had just been arrested.

Rhonda kept doing daredevil things, keeping her parents anxious even through her college years. All the while Nancy prayed for her daughter.

Rhonda had been born with a heart condition that caused a fast, erratic heartbeat, making it hard for her to breathe. When one these attacks hit her, she would have to go to the emergency room for an injection to regulate her heartbeat.

A few months ago, as she waited in the emergency room for a shot, conscious of the irregular beat of her heart, her mother's words came back to her. "Simply ask God. Simply ask God when you need Him." As the nurse was preparing the injection, Rhonda prayed silently and frantically, "Help me, God. Oh, help me." Suddenly her heart resumed beating normally. She asked the nurse to look at the monitor. It showed a normal heartbeat. She told the nurse she had just prayed and God had healed her.

Rhonda had tears in her eyes as she reported the incident to her mother. "God healed me. He really did!" she said. Later, when she came home for a high school class reunion, she told her parents she had rededicated her life to the Lord—after 23 years of her prodigal wanderings.

"My husband and I prayed every Scripture that remotely applied to her over those years," Nancy said. "And we just loved her. Our relationship the past few years had been very good, so we had opportunities to show her we loved her regardless of her status with God."

Came to Her Senses

I (Quin) was speaking at a Sunday morning service in Virginia when I stopped in the middle of the message and said something that surprised even me. "Someone here needs to hear this: Prodigals are going to start coming home . . . suddenly. Yours is one of them."

When I sat down, the lady sitting behind my front-row pew tapped me on the shoulder and said, "I think that word of encouragement was for me. I receive it. My prodigal is coming home!"

Within that very hour her daughter—living in a home for troubled teens due to drug abuse—sat down and wrote a letter. In it she asked for forgiveness and expressed a desire to come home and live a better life focused on God. A few days later she was released to return home and shortly afterwards asked Jesus to be her Lord. She joined a church youth group and now is being mentored by mature Christians. One of those mentors, a friend of the joyful mother, wrote to assure me that indeed the word I had spoken was fulfilled.

These stories should encourage any parent still in the waiting mode who is praying about a desperate prodigal situation. When life looks bleak, Scripture reminds us of God's promises to us: "We have this hope as an anchor for the soul, firm and secure. It enters the inner sanctuary behind the curtain, where Jesus, who went before us, has entered on our behalf" (Heb. 6:19,20).

Waiting for a prodigal to return is one of the most difficult experiences a parent may have to go through, but we can take comfort from the fact that God knows our distress and experiences it with us. In fact, Pastor Jack Hayford writes that God the Father, as well as His Son, suffered disappointment with those closest to them:

> If the infinitely loving, perfectly guided and excellently caring Father of all experienced a reversal of His hopes with an offspring, there is great hope available for any devoted parent wrestling with the haunting question that guilt recites over and over: "Where did I fail? . . ."
>
> Your straying child may have flown south and now winter's winds are trying to whip your soul to shreds. But I'm writing to encourage you to put on the garment of truth-filled praise. And to remember: When spring comes, those who "fly south" usually come back home. Expect that![8]

Prayer

Lord, thank You for the encouragement I get when I hear other people's victory stories. Help me not to be envious because my prodigal hasn't yet returned. You are a loving, impartial God, and I can trust You and Your timing. Help my unbelief when I need faith and strength to get through still another day of waiting. Show me how to encourage others who are also walking through heartache. May we begin to count our blessings instead of our losses. I'm so glad You are always calling our prodigals back to the Father's house. Please, Lord, keep calling! Amen.

Questions to Think About

1. In what areas of my life has God redeemed my own mistakes?
2. What is God's record of faithfulness in the life of my prodigal, even though I'm still waiting for his (her) return?

Notes
1. Tom Bisset, *Why Christian Kids Leave the Faith* (n.d.; reprint, Grand Rapids, MI: Discovery House, 1992), p. 206.
2. Lloyd Ogilvie, *A Future and a Hope* (Dallas: Word Publishing, 1988), p. 50.
3. Excerpts from newsletters of Barbara Johnson's Spatula Ministries, La Habra, CA.
4. Bisset, p. 207.
5. Franklin Graham, *Rebel With a Cause* (Nashville: Thomas Nelson, 1995), p. 314.
6. Edith Deen, *Great Women of the Christian Faith* (Westwood, NJ: Barbour and Co., 1959), p. 23.
7. Wesley L. Duewel, *Touch the World Through Prayer* (Grand Rapids, MI: Zondervan Publishing House, 1986), p. 93.
8. Jack Hayford, "When the Pastor's Kids Stray," *Ministries Today* (May/June 1999), p. 25.

CHAPTER ELEVEN

Hanging a "Welcome Home" Sign

Come to me, all you who are weary and burdened, and I will give you rest. Take my yoke upon you and learn from me, for I am gentle and humble in heart, and you will find rest for your souls. For my yoke is easy and my burden is light.

—MATTHEW 11:28-30

She walks into the terminal not knowing what to expect. Not one of the thousand scenes that have played out in her mind prepares her for what she sees. There, in the concrete-walls-and-

plastic-chairs bus terminal in Traverse City, Michigan, stands a
group of forty brothers and sisters and great-aunts and uncles
and cousins and a grandmother and great-grandmother to boot.
They're all wearing goofy party hats and blowing noise-makers,
and taped across the entire wall of the terminal is a
computer-generated banner that reads "Welcome home!"

Out of the crowd of well-wishers breaks her dad. She stares out
through the tears quivering in her eyes like hot mercury and
begins the memorized speech, "Dad, I'm sorry. I know . . ."

He interrupts her. "Hush, child. We've got no time for that.
No time for apologies. You'll be late for the party.
A banquet's waiting for you at home."[1]

—PHILIP YANCEY

An encouraging vignette from the life of Jesus is His treatment of Peter, the disciple who disowned him. In the emotionally charged hours following Jesus' arrest, Peter denied that he knew the Lord he had followed for three years. He even cursed to prove his point. Classic prodigal behavior.

But when the rooster crowed a second time, he came to himself. Remembering that Jesus had prophesied this would happen (see Mark 14:30), Peter wept tears of regret. How miserable he must have been during the following three days, carrying the guilt of his betrayal (see Mark 14:66-72).

After Jesus' crucifixion and burial, when the Sabbath was over, the women who had followed Jesus to the cross went to the tomb to anoint His body. But they found it empty! Their grief dissolved when a young man dressed in white announced to them that Jesus had risen from the dead. Then he gave specific instructions: "But go, tell his disciples *and Peter*, 'He is going ahead of you into Galilee. There you will see him, just as he told you' " (Mark 16:7, emphasis added).

Peter, the follower who turned his back on Jesus at the most critical moment, receives an invitation to meet with Jesus in Galilee. A "Welcome Home" sign is hung especially for him. Max Lucado writes:

> It's as if all of heaven had watched Peter fall—and it's as if all of heaven wanted to help him back up again. "Be sure and tell Peter that he's not left out. Tell him that one failure doesn't make a flop." . . . No wonder they call it the gospel of the second chance.[2]

Offering Acceptance

Have you hung a "Welcome Home" sign for your prodigal? Are you ready to give him or her a second chance? A third or a fourth? Maybe you've been so focused on praying he will *come to himself* that you haven't even thought about planning a welcome home party.

"They don't come home one day smelling like a pigpen and get up the next morning smelling like a rose—doing everything the way you'd like," one prodigal's mom told us.

Prodigals want to be accepted at face value for who they are, not because they measure up to keeping rules or adhering to behavior Christians expect of them. Part of the welcoming process is to allow them time to adjust. Here's where we need to ask God to establish them in godly friendships.

Some prodigals may say, "I love God, but I don't want to go to church." And you have to deal with

Prodigals want to be accepted at face value for who they are, not because they measure up to keeping rules or adhering to behavior Christians expect of them.

that. Considering their unique situations is a must—with their baggage of hurts, disappointments, lost dreams. Give them time, time, time to adjust. "I love you" is probably the sweetest phrase you can speak to them. "I forgive you" is probably the second-best sentence you can whisper.

"Many prodigals have come home only to find more rejection when they don't maintain perfection from the start," a former prodigal wrote us. "Often there is a process of healing. We have to be patient to allow the process the necessary time to bring results. Prodigals don't need to be reminded of how sinful their behavior is. They are usually painfully aware of how they don't measure up. They need to know that their dads and moms are willing to work with them and still love them even when failures have occurred."

Claiming My Son for God

We have heard numerous stories about the children of ministers who depart for the far country, leaving a wake of sorrow in the hearts of their parents. One pastor wrote and shared his own painful experience with a prodigal, which ultimately ended in joy:

I am a pastor and the father of a prodigal son. For a long time I lived in denial, not wanting to accept it. How could my son—*my* son—turn from the God I loved and had taught him to love? He began to rebel in his mid-teen years, but I kept a short leash on him, or so I thought. For both my children, I prayed and pointed them in the direction of fulfilling God's will for their lives.

After we moved to a different pastorate, things went from bad to worse in Mark's life. He dropped out of school sports activities, which he had always participated in, and yielded to the negative influences of other prodigals. Then he dropped out of high school only one semester before graduation. When he turned 18, he left home for his journey into the far country many miles away. He promised us he would find a church to attend, which he did at first. But then he met another prodigal, a young lady, and moved in with her. Soon they were both adrift.

The relationship lasted less than a year and he found himself alone and away from home. Even after he had been gone for about two years, I still would not admit to God or to myself that he was a genuine prodigal. Then, during the next two years, I was tested as never before when I finally faced the possibility that Mark may not return to God. Discouraged, I often wanted to resign as a pastor, though God was still using me to impact lives, and souls were being saved. Once I even wrote out my resignation, thinking this was God's direction for me.

Then I received a book in the mail: *How to Pray for Your Children*, by Quin Sherrer. Reading that book was a turning point. "I will not let the enemy have my son!" I declared. I made a commitment to God that daily I would pray and battle for Mark's soul. If it took until the day I died, I would not cease my prayers for him, claiming my son for God and asking Him to bring Mark to his senses. With that commitment I totally surrendered my son to the Lord. I determined to stay in contact with Mark, not preach to him, but to assure him, "Whatever you do, whatever you become, you will always be my son. You will always be loved, and every day I will see you in my prayers."

I worried that if Mark did not make a turnaround soon, his heart might become harder. But as I continued to humble myself before God, He revealed to me that along this difficult journey I was traveling, He was working in my life. I admit that I would not have learned some much-needed lessons had I not gone through this heartbreak.

One of the most important prayers to pray during a time like this is for God to send strong spiritual influences into our prodigal's life. This can serve to bring to remembrance all he has been taught and water all the spiritual seed that has been sown. If he could be so easily swayed by the negative influences, surely he might be won back by encounters with the positive.

Then, unexpectedly, Mark came to live with us for a while. He went out one night and met a girl at a drinking party and brought her home with him. When they both came into my house after 1:00 A.M., smelling of liquor, I angrily threw them out of the house. But after we turned out the lights, the Holy Spirit dealt with my heart as I overheard the two talking outside, sitting on the street curb. My heart melted as I thought how quickly I had judged.

I went out to talk with them and ended up inviting them back in to the stay the night (in separate bedrooms). The next morning Mark went to his job; after his new girlfriend got up, we talked and got better acquainted. I quickly discerned she had left a broken home and was very lonely with most of her family living in faraway England. As she shared more about her broken life, I told her about a loving heavenly Father who cares for her and was there to help. She then invited Jesus Christ into her heart and committed her life to Him.

They stayed on for a few days, but Mark quickly tired of our house rules. He would often vent his anger on us verbally, and finally they decided to go to England and live with her mother. After a few weeks, that situation became an emotional firestorm and they moved out. They found themselves with no money, no job and no food—in a far country indeed.

Meet in Heaven

This father goes on to tell the story of the week he was preparing to leave for a missions trip to Haiti. His son called him from England the night before his departure.

As Mark poured out his heart of discouragement and failure, I could do nothing but love and listen. I told him I was leaving for a remote part of Haiti the next day and would be out of communication with the family for 10 days. Then I said, "Son, I love you more than life, and I have not stopped praying for you. If something should happen to me and I not make it back home, please promise me—oh, please promise me, Son—you will meet me in heaven someday."

"Oh, Dad, nothing is going to happen to you," he protested.

But I asked him again to promise before we hung up that he would prepare to meet me in heaven. "Yes, Dad, I promise," he replied, almost crying.

The 10-day missions trip was an extensive time of prayer, fasting and ministry. The final Sunday, I preached in Port-au-Prince on the subject of the prodigal son. During that week, more than a hundred souls had come to Christ. On my way back home I wondered what had become of my dear son. Then I learned that somehow he and his girlfriend had gotten the money to return to the States and they flew in the same night I did. We were together again. I honestly had not known whether I would ever see him again in this life.

During that week I talked to Mark's girlfriend several times and was thrilled that the good seed was still in her heart. We prayed and shared the Bible. Then came Sunday morning. I looked out and saw a sight I had almost despaired of ever seeing—Mark and his girlfriend were sitting together in my church for worship. The Lord spoke powerfully through His Word and His Spirit that morning, and I gave an invitation. My son's girlfriend came to the altar—and following close behind was Mark! I fell on my knees at the altar and prayed with them as they both repented and gave their lives to God. I thought I was dreaming—nothing else in all the world mattered at that moment as much as my son, and I hugged him for several minutes, his shoulder bathed in my tears—tears of joy for such a merciful God who had brought the prodigal home.

"Come sing with me—praise God with me," I said, turning to the congregation. "Rejoice with me! My son which was dead is alive. My son which was lost is now found!" And we all began to make merry. Two weeks later they both were baptized, and now they plan to marry and serve the Lord together.

Coming Home

For Rebecca, the welcome home given her son was a long time coming, but it was worth waiting for. Early in life, her son Morris developed a victim mentality because of his father's abusive treatment. After a painful divorce, Rebecca married a man who later became a pastor, but the emotional damage to her son began to take a toll. When Morris reached his teen years he started running from God, got involved with drugs and then suffered a wrecked marriage. Unable to feel loved and accepted for who he was, he left for the "far country" and sought acceptance anywhere he could find it.

"I asked every intercessor I could to pray for my son," Rebecca said. "After his marriage failed he had a breakdown, but still he was a prodigal. For years my friends continued soaking him with prayer from afar. When he finally came home at age 37, his stepdad received him with love. 'Get well, get whole, Morris,' he told him. 'You don't have to get a job right now. Your mom and I are here to see that you are restored.' "

Morris did get well, and later he was able to find a job. One of Rebecca's best friends and longtime prayer partners deliberately went to work at the place where he was hired. Her goal: to continue interceding for this prodigal and calling forth his inheritance. Now promoted to a supervisory position, Morris freely asks for prayer. His mother's friend prays with him every day at work, and occasionally they spend their lunch break doing a Bible study.

Because of unresolved areas in his life, stemming from childhood, Morris had always had trouble keeping a job. If a boss seemed too demanding, it made him recall his father's harsh ways, and he would either quit or get fired. But he's begun to identify these problems and is asking God to heal him. Now drug and alcohol free, Morris is growing in the Lord, sharing a house with his brother and settling down to enjoy life.

At age 39 he wrote his stepdad a letter saying, "The best thing that happened to me was coming home. Thanks for taking such good care of my mom—and me. Love, Morris."

What was the key to this prodigal's return? Certainly the prayers of friends who continued to pray for him without judging him were a major factor. But the love and acceptance of a stepdad who invited him home without the strain of having to work was crucial to his becoming whole again.

The father in Jesus' parable saw his son coming "while he was still a long way off" (Luke 15:20). He ran to meet him, smothering him with kisses even before the rebel asked for his forgiveness. What a pattern this is for us. If you are praying for a prodigal child to return, ask the Holy Spirit to show you ways you can assure your child that the "Welcome Home" sign is out.

Life Is Precious

When Bernice and Tim learned their 15-year-old daughter, Cheryl, was expecting a baby, Tim thought abortion was the best solution because Cheryl was so young and had a promising life ahead.

Until this happened, Bernice really didn't know where she stood on the abortion issue. Then she talked to a pastor who clearly explained his position and read her these verses: "For you created my inmost being; you knit me together in my mother's womb. I praise you because I am fearfully and wonderfully made; your works are wonderful, I know that full well" (Ps. 139:13,14).

"The pastor convinced me that life is precious and that God has a plan for each person," she said. "I realized that God knows us intimately from conception and that a baby is a *life* even then—not just a clump of cells or a blob of tissue." Bernice went home and told her husband she would not participate in helping Cheryl get an abortion—she would only help to care for her afterward.

Tim insisted he wanted what was best for his daughter, but he pressed Cheryl to make a decision soon. Meanwhile, Bernice's close Christian friends were praying that Cheryl would make the choice God wanted her to make. Tim, impatient with her indecision, went ahead and made an appointment for the procedure to be done.

On the afternoon scheduled for the abortion, a friend of Bernice's brought her three-year-old toddler for a visit. "I really believe abortion is wrong, Cheryl," she said. "If you decide not to have one, I know a Christian family who would love to adopt your baby. Please consider it."

Cheryl played with the friend's toddler for a while and then went to her bedroom for some time alone. When her dad came to get her for the clinic appointment, she hung her head and said, "Dad, I can't. I just can't have an abortion."

Shocked and angry, Tim packed his bags and moved out of the house for two weeks. Cheryl went to an out-of-state

Christian home for unwed mothers and asked that her baby be given to a childless Christian couple.

After the baby was born, Bernice and Tim had the joy of holding her. They held her once more six weeks later when they returned with Cheryl to sign the adoption release papers. Cheryl moved back home and finished high school. One day she told Bernice, "Mom, if I'd had the abortion, I'd probably be back drinking and looking for acceptance."

But Cheryl didn't adjust well; she felt such a void in her life—missing her baby and wishing for someone to love her. When an older man came along and swept her off her feet, she moved onto a houseboat with him. She got a job and virtually supported the two of them. They did get married. But a year later when he kicked her off the boat, she called her parents to come get her.

Getting Her Life in Order

All this time Bernice and her friends were praying for this prodigal daughter to turn back to God and to her family. Cheryl moved back home, filed for divorce and began getting her life back in order. She soon realized she needed a better education, so she worked in the daytime and attended college at night.

A major key to Cheryl's restoration was knowing she could return home when trouble hit. The welcome mat was out. The welcome mat is still out. With her parents' help, she is pursuing her dream of attending law school and becoming an attorney. Jesus is her firm rock now, and there is no turning back.

Quin's Prodigal Returned

Last year, our former Florida pastor, Peter Lord, visited us in Colorado. Our son, Keith, and his family were living with us after just finishing seven years of service with Youth With A Mission (YWAM).

As they sat on the couch talking, Keith said, "Pastor, I used to sit in the back of the church with the rest of the youth. When you asked those who wanted to give their hearts to the Lord to come down to the altar for prayer, I wouldn't go. My palms would sweat. I'd say to myself, *If I made such a decision, I'm sure God would make me go to Africa. No, I'm not going to Africa.*

"Pastor Lord, I just want you to know I've been to Africa twice on a mercy ship for YWAM. I thought about you and all the sermons I'd heard you preach. You see, I did make a decision for Jesus."

Pastor Lord grinned and put an arm about Keith's shoulder. He was probably remembering the times he'd prayed with us for our son, as we declared him a "mighty man of God," when his circumstances at the moment were not that positive.

While Keith's years of missions travels are over, he now has his own graphic arts business, something he studied in college and loves to do.

God uses our youngsters' talents and skills in various seasons of their lives if we parents release them from our expectations. I remember how I relinquished my children to God and said, "God, this child is Yours. My heart and home are open." The time came, after their prodigal days were over, when all three of our children lived overseas—in different countries—at the same time.

Will the welcome mat be out for your child if he or she chooses a career you don't like? Marries someone you don't approve of? Moves to a country far removed from you? It's a matter of keeping an open heart as well as an open home.

Covenant-Keeping God

God often refers to Himself as a covenant-keeping God. But a covenant is a two-way agreement. He says, "I will, if you will." Once I (Quin) heard a visiting preacher tell a group of Bible school students a personal story about covenant that illustrates this.

His daughter married and had two girls. Then his daughter learned her husband was unfaithful, and the marriage fell apart. She was mad at God for letting it happen and mad at her dad for not stopping her from marrying the man. Estranged from her family, she didn't even let her folks see their grandchildren. And she certainly didn't go to church. Her father doubted she ever told her daughters about the loving God he preached about every Sunday.

Years passed and the girls reached their teens. Now financially strapped, the daughter humbled herself and asked her parents for help. How thrilled they were to at least have contact with her again. They moved a mobile home onto their property; now they could get to know their granddaughters.

One day the preacher came home from a trip and bounded up the steps of the mobile home to see his grandchildren. Inside he heard a loud conversation going on, so he hesitated and listened.

"Why is it we suddenly have to start reading the Bible and talk about going to church?" one teen shouted at her mom. "You've never cared about religious things before."

"Well, God has a covenant with your granddaddy—and we can't get out of it," she shouted back.

"A covenant—what's that?" the teen asked.

The pastor quickly retreated down the stairs, not wanting to interrupt the conversation. He concluded the story by telling the Bible school students, "My daughter isn't yet in the place I desire her to be spiritually, but she and the girls are on the way. It's a start. I'm trusting God to keep His covenant with me for our family."

Here are just two verses about covenant, from among almost 300 references found in Scripture:

> Know therefore that the LORD your God is God; he is the faithful God, keeping his covenant of love to a thousand generations of those who love him and keep his commands (Deut. 7:9).

> "As for me, this is my covenant with them," says the LORD. "My Spirit, who is on you, and my words that I have put in your mouth will not depart from your mouth, or from the mouths of your children, or from the mouths of their descendants from this time on and forever," says the LORD (Isa. 59:21).

God Cares About Families

Salvation for the entire household was God's plan—and it continues to be His plan—for our families.

When God told Noah to go into the ark, his entire family of eight was included; all were spared in the flood (see Gen. 7:1).

When Rahab the harlot hid the Israelite spies in Jericho, she was offered protection for herself and all her father's family (Josh. 2:12-19).

Cornelius, the first Gentile believer, accepted salvation when Peter preached in his home, and his relatives and close friends also believed and were baptized (see Acts 11:4-18).

Lydia became Paul's first European convert, and she and her household were saved (see Acts 16:13-15).

Paul said to the jailer in Philippi, "Believe in the Lord Jesus, and you will be saved—you and your household" (Acts 16:31). Paul told him about the Lord and "he was filled with joy because he had come to believe in God—he and his whole family" (v. 34).

Going to Heaven

My (Quin's) friend, whom I'll call Jackie, traveled northward from her home in the South each summer to attend her family reunion. Year after year she did this. She was one of a few in her extremely large family of siblings, aunts, uncles and cousins who was a Christian. For years she had prayed for their salvation, with no tangible sign of victory. Then last summer she went once again.

As they casually sat around visiting one afternoon, one of Jackie's sisters stood up and said, "These reunions are such fun I think we should continue them someday in heaven. But we had all better be sure we're going there. Jackie, would you come up here and pray with all of us so we can go to heaven and attend another family reunion there?"

Jackie was shocked at first, but honored. She rose from her chair and stood beside her sister in front of the crowd.

"Well, praying for salvation is special, but it is not just so we can go to heaven," she explained. "It is special for here on earth, too. Jesus came to give us life abundant. Salvation includes healing, safety and protection also. So will you all just pray aloud with me?

"Father, I come to You, admitting I need Jesus as my Savior. I ask for Your forgiveness, mercy, peace and direction in my life. I am sorry for ways I've disappointed You. . . . I want to turn around. . . ."

She continued leading them in a prayer to surrender their wills to His will and purpose. Forty of her relatives came to the Lord that day! Her longtime prayers for these lost but beloved relatives were answered suddenly on an ordinary afternoon.[3]

We have no idea how long it may take for a prodigal to decide to come home. But as we pray, we can remind God of His covenant with us and ask Him to overwhelm the prodigal with His love. God does care about families and He is always ready to say, "Welcome home!"

Softly and Tenderly

Toward the end of the nineteenth century, Dwight L. Moody conducted large evangelistic meetings in which thousands came to Christ. At the close of his message, the song "Softly and Tenderly" often was sung as he gave an invitation.

When the evangelist lay on his deathbed, the composer of the song, Will Thompson, visited his friend one last time. Mr. Moody commended the hymn writer for composing the song, and a short time later entered his eternal rest with these words of invitation once again upon his lips:[4]

Softly and tenderly Jesus is calling
Calling for you and for me.
See, on the portals he's waiting and watching,
Watching for you and for me.

O for the wonderful love he has promised,
Promised for you and for me.
Though we have sinned, he has mercy and pardon,
Pardon for you and for me.

Come home, come home,
You who are weary, come home.
Earnestly, tenderly, Jesus is calling,
Calling, O sinner, come home!

—Will L. Thompson (1849-1909)

Catherine Marshall wrote, "The Lord is in the business of restoring broken homes and healing damaged families. . . . He is the God of redemption and new beginnings."[5]

Yes, and He is also the God who redeems our mistakes. Therefore, we can have hope that every wandering prodigal will respond to His call, "Come home!"

Prayer

Dear heavenly Father, the thought of being able to welcome home my prodigal thrills me. Strengthen my faith so I'll be steadfast in prayer until it happens. Help me to have a heart like that of the prodigal's father in the Bible—always watching for _____'s return, always ready to welcome, embrace and forgive. Lord, give me the ability to communicate Your love to my prodigal, no matter what the circumstances may be. Thank You, Father, for Your mercy and Your faithfulness. Amen.

Questions to Think About

1. Am I willing to relinquish my expectation of how and when I want my prodigal's return to happen?
2. Can I accept my son for who he is, even with shaggy, unkempt hair, crude manners and the stench of the pigpen still on his clothes? Or my daughter with tattoos, body piercings and spiked purple hair? Can I see beyond the "externals" and believe God for a heart change?

Notes

1. Taken from *What's So Amazing About Grace?* by Philip Yancey. Copyright © 1997 by Philip D. Yancey. Used by permission of Zondervan Publishing House, p. 46.
2. Max Lucado, *No Wonder They Call Him the Savior* (Portland: Multnomah Press, 1986), p. 44.
3. Adapted from *Good Night, Lord* © 2000 by Quin Sherrer, p. 18. Published by Regal Books, Ventura, California. Used with permission.
4. Kenneth W. Osbeck, ed., *Amazing Grace: 366 Inspiring Hymn Stories for Daily Devotions* (Grand Rapids, MI: Kregel Publications, 1990), p. 184.
5. Catherine Marshall, *Light in My Darkest Night* (Grand Rapids, MI: Baker Book House, 1989), p. 27.

Three days after Quin and I met with the directors of Regal and agreed to write this book, I attended a women's luncheon with a friend. When I told her our ideas for *Praying Prodigals Home*, she related her own experience of praying for her wayward son. He has since renewed his relationship with the Lord and recently married a beautiful Christian girl.

Then she shared this vignette from the days of her son's stay at a men's rehab ranch in Alabama for drug addicts. One of her son's roommates was struggling with the strictness of the program and decided to drop out. Late one night, unable to sleep, he went out on the pier at the edge of a nearby lake.

"God, get out of my life!" he screamed in frustration as he paced back and forth. "I can't take it anymore. Just leave me alone, okay?"

In the quiet darkness he heard a still, small voice speaking to his heart: *I'll leave you alone when your mama leaves Me alone!*

The young man began to weep, realizing his mother's prayers had pursued him through all the years of his rebellion. He went back to the dorm and the next day told his counselor he was ready to make things right with God. He wanted to stay in the program until he truly was free.

What a faith booster to know that when we ask God to intervene in our prodigals' lives, He works in all kinds of ways to get their attention.

During the last few days of working on this book, I called Barbara, a friend whose story appears in chapter 1, to get an update on her 26-year-old prodigal daughter, Carlyn. This young woman had finally broken free from an abusive relationship and returned home, but at last report she had not yet reconciled her relationship with the Lord.

Barbara told me Carlyn is now involved with another man who abuses her and tries to control her. Not long ago she came home bloody after being beaten by him, but she won't press charges and she's still in the relationship. It's been hard for Barbara to hold on to her faith in light of Carlyn's behavior. We prayed together on the phone, and I promised to solicit additional prayer support.

A few days later she called with a good report. Carlyn had taken her shopping and the two enjoyed some quality time together. At one point her daughter said, "Mom, you don't need to worry about me believing in God. I do believe in Him—I just don't like going to church."

"That's not the complete breakthrough I'm praying for, but it's a huge step for her to tell me that," Barbara said. "She doesn't curse in my presence anymore, her heart is tender toward me, and she's spending more time at home. I'm so grateful for this change in her—it gives me hope to keep praying."

I reminded Barbara that when Carlyn says hurtful things to her, she mustn't take it personally and feel so wounded that she gives up. "It's the *enemy* who motivates your daughter to say those things to hurt you so you'll get discouraged and stop praying," I said. "Just keep loving your daughter, praying and resisting the enemy." Again, we prayed a prayer of agreement for Carlyn, and I assured Barbara I'm standing with her in agreement until total victory comes.

I realized anew how counterproductive it is for us to expect prodigals to attend church when their hearts aren't yet ready. Many of them believe they will only be rejected by people in church anyway, so why bother to go? As in the parable—first the prodigal must come to himself; *then* he's ready to go to the

Father's house. I also realized how important it is for intercessors to encourage one another in the face of despair over praying for prodigals.

May this book give you a new lease on hope and cause you to renew your commitment to pray and not give up.

Yes—God hears your prayers.

Yes—He is working in the unseen realm, influencing circumstances in your prodigal's life and sending laborers across his or her path.

Yes—your prayers make a difference.

Yes—it's always too soon to quit!

—Ruthanne Garlock

I urge ... that requests, prayers, intercession and thanksgiving be made for everyone. . . . This is good, and pleases God our Savior, who wants all men to be saved and to come to a knowledge of the truth (1 Tim. 2:1,3,4).

Waging Your Prayer Battle

Interceding in prayer for the prodigal we want to see rescued is only part of what is needed. We also need to battle against opposing spiritual forces. We direct our prayers to God, and our spiritual warfare toward the enemy.

Some may be afraid of the term "spiritual warfare." But it is a scriptural principle we see modeled in the life of Jesus. Following His baptism, when Jesus encountered Satan during the wilderness temptation, He overcame the enemy by quoting the Word of God (see Luke 4:1-14). In His teaching, Jesus made many references to the devil (for examples see Matt. 4:3; 6:13;

12:24-26; 25:41; John 8:44; 10:10). And in praying for His followers, Jesus asked the Father to "protect them from the evil one" (John 17:15).

Let's take a look at the basic principles of spiritual warfare, beginning with awareness of the enemy.

Know the Enemy

Satan is God's enemy and ours. Scripture says: "Be sober, be vigilant; because your adversary the devil walks about like a roaring lion, seeking whom he may devour. Resist him, steadfast in the faith" (1 Pet. 5:8,9, *NKJV*).

The prodigal we are praying for is not the enemy—he or she is the one Satan seeks to devour. Unbelievers who are blinded and manipulated by Satan may behave like enemies, but they are not (see 2 Cor. 10:4). Sometimes even well-meaning believers may behave like enemies, but we must not be deceived into battling against flesh and blood. We must always direct our spiritual warfare toward Satan and his emissaries.

Battle in the Spiritual Realm

Paul wrote, "For we are not fighting against people made of flesh and blood, but against persons without bodies—the evil rulers of the unseen world" (Eph. 6:12, *TLB*). These unseen powers do wield influence and they target God's people (see Dan. 10:12-14; Mark 4:15; 8:33; Luke 22:3,31,32; John 8:44; Acts 5:3; 26:18; 2 Cor. 2:11; 4:4; 1 Thess. 2:18).

The devil will try to distract us by causing us to respond to people and circumstances in the flesh. But an astute spiritual warrior understands how the enemy works and recognizes that the battle is in the spiritual realm, not the natural realm.

These are some of the enemy's most basic tactics:

1. He tries to destroy believers' confidence in God and His Son, so they will forsake the faith.
2. He tries to seduce believers through deceptive teaching or their own sin to believe a lie instead of the truth.
3. He tries to prevent unbelievers from hearing a clear presentation of the gospel, so they will remain in Satan's kingdom.
4. He tries to intensify the pressure and stress on believers in an effort to wear them out and cause them to give up hope that anything will ever change (see 1 Cor. 16:9).

Ask for a Strategy

The Holy Spirit is our divine intelligence agent for the spiritual conflict we're engaged in. As we study the battles in the Old Testament, we discover that God gave clear instructions for each one—that is, when the people sought His direction. (A few references for study are Joshua 5:13–6:27; Judges 4,6,7; 1 Samuel 7:2-17; 14:1-23; 17; 30; 2 Chronicles 20.)

We must ask for guidance from the Holy Spirit for strategy in our battles and learn to recognize His voice as we seek to know Him better. Sometimes we may hear the voice of the enemy or we may hear the voice of our own human desire and reasoning. These possibilities can lead to deception. Of course the Lord can choose to speak to us in an audible voice, but that rarely happens. Usually He speaks in more subtle ways—for example, through

- verses of Scripture,
- biblical teaching we hear,
- words of encouragement and direction from others,
- a song that comes to mind or one we hear on the radio or in church,
- an incident that happens,
- something we observe in nature,
- a still, small voice we hear in our thoughts.

Probably our most important strategy is to make sure we harbor no unforgiveness or bitterness in our hearts toward anyone. Often the prodigal we're praying for is the very one who causes us to feel disappointment, hurt and anger. Or we may be angry with another person who we feel is somehow responsible for the situation. The enemy tries to convince us our anger is justified, for he knows anger nullifies our prayers and warfare. Paul clearly warns us: "Do not let the sun go down while you are still angry, and do not give the devil a foothold" (Eph. 4:26,27; see also 2 Cor. 2:10,11).

Choosing to forgive is an act of the will—it may take time before our emotions come into agreement with our decision. Once we take the first step toward forgiveness, we can count on God to provide the strength to help us. God always rewards our obedience to His Word. But if we don't forgive, we block God's flow of forgiveness to us and thus hinder our own prayers (see Mark 11:25,26).

When we choose to forgive someone, we cut ourselves free from bondage and we commit the person into God's hand for

His mercy and judgment. Thus we're in a position to effectively pray and wage warfare for that person.

Use Our Weapons

Following is a review of the most basic weapons available to us for waging spiritual warfare:

The Name of Jesus

His name has power to defeat the enemy because of Christ's sacrificial death on the cross. But we can only use His name with authority when we are in right relationship with Him—when there's no unforgiveness or hidden sin in our hearts and when we're walking in faith and obedience.

Jesus told His followers: "I have given you authority . . . to overcome all the power of the enemy" (Luke 10:19). We pray in the name of Jesus and we speak aloud to make declarations to the enemy in the name of Jesus. Singing songs about the power of Jesus' name is another way to declare victory. (Other references to power in the name of Jesus are Psalm 44:5,6; Mark 16:17; Luke 9:1,2; John 14:13,14; Acts 19:13-17; Philippians 2:9,10.)

The Blood of Jesus

Jesus' blood—the means of our redemption—is the most precious substance on Earth (see 1 Pet. 1:18-21). He was completely without sin, yet He chose to die a sacrificial death to atone for all the sins of mankind (see Rom. 5:12-17). When Jesus went to the cross and shed His blood, He sealed Satan's defeat and stripped him of his weapons (see Col. 2:13-15).

To declare the blood of Jesus over a person is a way of giving notice to the enemy that Jesus' blood is a boundary he cannot permanently violate. This is based on Exodus 12:23. The blood of a lamb applied to the doorposts and lintels of the houses of God's people protected their firstborn from the death angel who struck down and killed the firstborn in all the Egyptian households.

Prayers of Agreement

Jesus said, "If two of you on earth agree about anything you ask for, it will be done for you by my Father in heaven. For where two or three come together in my name, there am I with them" (Matt. 18:19,20).

As intercessors and spiritual warriors we must first agree with the Holy Spirit and His purposes, for our prayers to be answered. Once we have the Holy Spirit's direction as to how to pray, we can see greater effectiveness when we pray in agreement with another intercessor. To agree means to be in harmony or without contention. When two of us pray in agreement with the Holy Spirit, we establish a "threefold cord" that is not easily broken (see Eccles. 4:9-12, *NKJV*).

Binding and Loosing

Jesus said to His followers: "No one can enter a strong man's house and plunder his goods, unless he first binds the strong man. And then he will plunder his house" (Mark 3:27, *NKJV*; see also Matt. 16:19; Luke 11:21,22).

To bind evil spirits means to restrain them—to forbid them to continue their destructive activity in the life of the individual.

We address the spirits directly. Then through the power of the Holy Spirit we declare the person is loosed from the enemy's bondage. In prayer we ask the Father to send the Holy Spirit to minister according to the person's need. Here's an example of such a prayer:

> *Father, thank You that You have given us the power through Christ to take authority over the works of the evil one. By that authority we bind all lying, unclean, rebellious, God-hating, antichrist spirits that are operating in _____'s life right now. We declare their assignments against _____ are rendered null and void through the blood of Christ, our Savior, who won the victory through His death on the cross. We release _____ from the influence of these evil spirits. We ask the Holy Spirit to reveal truth, and we call _____ to repentance.*

Fasting

Fasting—a voluntary abstinence from food—is a powerful warfare tool. God declares its purpose: "Is not this the kind of fasting I have chosen: to loose the chains of injustice and untie the cords of the yoke, to set the oppressed free and break every yoke?" (Isa. 58:6).

Fasting is not an arm-twisting technique to try to convince God to do things our way. We can use this effective spiritual weapon for several purposes:

1. To sharpen our sensitivity to the Holy Spirit
2. To seek the Lord's strategy for our battle
3. To allow more time for Bible study—Scripture often comes alive to us during fasting
4. To break the strongholds of the enemy

Because of medical reasons, not everyone can abstain completely from food. But there are some things we can fast—maybe certain foods, sleep, television or other entertainment. Some can do a "Daniel fast"—eat no meat and only a minimal amount of very common foods (see Dan. 10:2). Others fast from solid food but take liquids such as water and clear juices. The point is to set aside time for prayer and seeking God during the time of the fast (see also 2 Chron. 20:3; Matt. 6:16-18; Luke 4:1,2,14; Acts 14:23).

Praise

Perhaps you have not considered praise as a spiritual weapon, but Psalm 149:6-8 verifies that it is: "May the praise of God be in their [the saints'] mouths and a double-edged sword in their hands, to inflict vengeance on the nations, . . . to bind their kings with fetters, their nobles with shackles of iron." We think of "nations" and "nobles" as being principalities and powers in the demonic realm.

We battle from a position of victory, since God has already put all things under Jesus' feet (see Eph. 1:19-22). Through praise, Jehoshaphat's army sent confusion to the ranks of the enemy, and Paul and Silas were released from prison (see 2 Chron. 20:14-22; Acts 16:23-26).

We can offer praises by singing of God's almighty power and Jesus' defeat of Satan, by our own declarations of praise and by proclaiming aloud the promises from Scripture that assure God's victory.

The Word of God

Everything we do in spiritual warfare must be firmly based on God's Word—the sword of the Spirit. God says, "So is my word that goes out from my mouth: It will not return to me empty, but will accomplish what I desire and achieve the purpose for which I sent it" (Isa. 55:11). We declare His Word—not our own desires or ideas in a matter—to see God's purposes fulfilled (see also Eph. 6:17; Heb. 4:12). Here are four ways to use this weapon of warfare:

1. Ask the Lord to quicken in your heart a specific verse(s) to use as a weapon.
2. Declare the Word aloud to the enemy to remind him of his defeat.
3. Speak the Word aloud to the Lord, affirming that you are standing on His promise.
4. Allow the Holy Spirit to speak through the Word with encouragement, guidance or correction.

Here's an example of using the Word for both prayer and warfare. This example uses just two verses of Scripture: 2 Timothy 2:25b,26 (NASB).

God, grant _____ repentance that leads to the knowledge of the truth, that he (she) may come to his (her) senses and escape from the snare of the devil, having been held captive by him to do his will.

Using the same verses for warfare, you wield the sword of the Spirit to speak aloud to the enemy, just as Jesus did when the devil tested Him:

Satan, the Word of God says that you have my prodigal held captive to do your will. So in the name and by the authority of Jesus Christ of Nazareth, whom I serve, I tell you to loose his (her) will, so he (she) will be free to choose to follow Jesus.

Here's another example of praying God's Word over the person for whom you're interceding, based on Psalms 34:7; 91:3,11,15 *(NKJV)*:

Thank You, Lord, for Your promise that the angel of the Lord encamps around those who fear You, and he delivers them. I'm trusting you to deliver _____ from every trap of the evil one. Lord, please give Your angels charge over _____ to keep him (her) in all his ways. Thank you that _____ will call upon You, and You will be with him (her) in trouble. Amen.

Why People Don't Come to the Lord

Here are some scriptural reasons why some people don't come to the Lord or why they backslide into becoming prodigals:

1. Satan has held them captive to do his will (see 2 Tim. 2:25,26).
2. Satan has blinded them. "But even if our gospel is veiled, it is veiled to those who are perishing, whose minds the god of this age has blinded, who do not believe, lest the light of the gospel of the glory of Christ, who is the image of God, should shine on them" (2 Cor. 4:3,4, *NKJV*).
3. The worries of this world, the deceitfulness of riches and the desire for other things choke out the Word of God (see Mark 4:19).

4. They harbor unforgiveness. Paul said, "I have forgiven in the sight of Christ for your sake, in order that Satan might not outwit us. For we are not unaware of his schemes" (2 Cor. 2:10,11).

5. There are not enough harvesters in the field (see Matt. 9:37,38).

Godly Goals

Here are scriptural goals you may want to incorporate in your prayers for your children:

1. That Jesus Christ be formed in them (see Gal. 4:19)

2. That they—the seed of the righteous—will be delivered from the evil one (see Prov. 11:21, *KJV*; Matt. 6:13)

3. That they will be taught of the Lord and their peace will be great (see Isa. 54:13)

4. That they will train themselves to discern good from evil and have a good conscience toward God (see Heb. 5:14; 1 Pet. 3:21)

5. That God's laws will be in their minds and on their hearts (see Heb. 8:10)

6. That they will choose companions who are wise—not fools—being neither sexually immoral, drunkards, idolaters, slanderers nor swindlers (see Prov. 13:20; 1 Cor. 5:11)

7. That they will remain sexually pure and keep themselves only for their spouse, asking for God's grace to keep such a commitment (see Eph. 5:3,31,33)

8. That they will honor their parents (see Eph. 6:1-3)[1]

Praying Against Evil Influences

Here are suggestions for prayer regarding a child who is being adversely influenced by peers:

1. God may lead you to pray as David did when he believed his son Absalom was hearing the wrong advice. He asked the Lord to "turn [the] counsel into foolishness" (2 Sam. 15:31).
2. God may lead you to pray that your child be "delivered from wicked and evil men" and that He "strengthen and protect [him (her)] from the evil one" (2 Thess. 3:2,3).
3. God may want you to bless that person, even when your natural inclination is to ask God to remove his harmful influence from your child's life. You can pray that God will accomplish His plan and purpose in that person, bringing the right people into his or her life at the right time (see Matt. 9:38; Eph. 1:11). God broke Job's captivity when he prayed for his friends, and they weren't exactly the kind of friends most of us would want (see Job 42:10).[2]

Salvation Prayer for a Prodigal

The greatest event in history made it possible for every prodigal to come home to the Father. Jesus, God's Son, came to Earth and took the blame for the sins of our pride, rebellion and selfishness, which separated all mankind from God. He loved us even in our rebellion and died on the cross to pay the penalty for our sins.

After three days in the grave, Jesus rose from the dead—securing His promise that we, too, can have eternal life. We need only confess and repent of our sins, receive His forgiveness and acknowledge Him as Lord. By praying the following prayer, anyone can be reconciled to God the Father and freely approach Him with every need by praying in Jesus' name.

> *Lord Jesus, I confess I am a sinner who has wandered away from Your love. I repent for my sin and my rebellion against You. Please forgive me for walking in my own selfish ways, and wash me clean. I receive You as my Lord and Savior. I believe You are the Son of God who came to earth, died on the cross, shed Your blood for my sins and rose from the dead. Lord, strengthen me to live my life in a way that is pleasing to You. Father God, thank You that the gift of salvation through Your Son makes it possible for me to pray to You in Jesus' name. I rejoice in Your promise that I will live with You forever in heaven. Amen.*

Praying the Scriptures

In chapter 2 we mentioned Jean and her daughter who had lost her faith. Believing that her daughter will one day return, Jean prays for her daughter. Her prayers are based on Ezekiel 36:25-36 *(NLT)* and Colossians 1:9-12 *(NIV)*.

> *I will sprinkle clean water on you, _____, and you will be clean. Your filth will be washed away, and you will no longer worship idols. And I will give you a new heart with new and right*

desires, and I will put a new spirit in you. I will take out your stony heart of sin and give you a new, obedient heart. And I will put my Spirit in you so you will obey my laws and do whatever I command. You will be my people, and I will be your God. I will cleanse you of your filthy behavior. I will give you great harvests. This is what the Sovereign LORD says: "When I cleanse you from your sins, I will bring people to live in your cities, and the ruins will be rebuilt. The [spiritual] fields that used to lie empty and desolate—a shock to all who passed by—will again be farmed. And when I bring you back, people will say, 'This godforsaken land is now like Eden's garden!' . . . I, the LORD, have promised this, and I will do it."

We have not stopped praying for you, _____, and asking God to fill you with the knowledge of his will through all spiritual wisdom and understanding. And we pray this in order that you may live a life worthy of the Lord and may please him in every way: bearing fruit in every good work, growing in the knowledge of God, being strengthened with all power according to his glorious might so that you may have great endurance and patience, and joyfully giving thanks to the Father, who has qualified you to share in the inheritance of the saints in the kingdom of light.

Notes

1. From *The Spiritual Warrior's Prayer Guide* © 1992 by Quin Sherrer and Ruthanne Garlock. Published by Servant Publications, Box 8617, Ann Arbor, Michigan, 48107, pp. 158, 159. Used with permission.
2. Ibid., pp. 157, 158.

Authority over the enemy:
Isaiah 44:25-26a; 54:17; 55:11; 59:19
Jeremiah 1:12
Matthew 10:8; 12:28,29; 16:19
Mark 3:27; 6:7; 16:17
Luke 10:19
2 Corinthians 2:14
Ephesians 1:19-22; 4:8; 6:10-18
Colossians 2:15
Revelation 1:18

For protection:
Deuteronomy 28:6,7
Psalms 5:11; 7:7-9; 91:1-10
Proverbs 2:8
Isaiah 54:17

Restoration and security:
Psalms 31:8; 32:7
Proverbs 10:30; 12:3,21; 18:10
Joel 2:18-32

For strength and declaration of victory:
1 Samuel 17:45
2 Samuel 22:33,35,40
2 Kings 6:16,17
Psalms 18:29; 68:28; 149:6-9
Song of Solomon 6:10
Isaiah 41:15; 50:7
Jeremiah 12:5; 23:29

For healing:
Exodus 15:26
Psalm 103:3
Proverbs 3:7,8; 4:20-22
Isaiah 53:5
Matthew 4:23; 9:28,29; 15:26-28
Luke 9:11
1 Peter 2:24
1 John 3:8

For children:
Psalms 91; 127:3-5; 144:12
Isaiah 43:5; 49:25; 54:13; 59:21
Jeremiah 29:11-14; 31:16,17
Joel 2:25-29
Malachi 4:6
Colossians 1:9-12

Dealing with an abusive person:
Psalms 31:20,21; 32:7; 37; 144:11; 145:18
Ezekiel 28:24-26

For guidance:
Psalms 34:19; 37:23,24; 123:1,2
Proverbs 3:5,6
Isaiah 30:21
2 Corinthians 5:7

For provision and finances:
Leviticus 26:3-13
Deuteronomy 8:7-10,18
1 Kings 17:2-4,8,9
2 Chronicles 15:7; 32:8
Malachi 3:10,11
Matthew 6:25,32
Luke 6:38

RECOMMENDED READING

Bisset, Tom. *Why Christian Kids Leave the Faith*. N.d. Reprint, Grand Rapids, MI: Discovery House, 1992.

Dawson, Joy. *Intercession: Thrilling and Fulfilling*. Seattle: YWAM Publishing, 1997.

Dobson, Dr. James C. *Parenting Isn't for Cowards*. Dallas: Word Publishing, 1987.

Eastman, Dick. *Love on Its Knees*. Tarrytown, NY: Fleming H. Revell, 1989.

Fuller, Cheri. *When Children Pray*. Sisters, OR: Multnomah Publishers, 1997.

_____. *When Mothers Pray*. Sisters, OR: Multnomah Publishers, 1999.

Graham, Franklin. *Rebel With a Cause*. Nashville: Thomas Nelson Publishers, 1995.

Graham, Ruth Bell. *Prodigals and Those Who Love Them*. Colorado Springs: Focus on the Family, 1991.

Jacobs, Cindy. *Possessing the Gates of the Enemy*. Grand Rapids, MI: Baker Book House, 1991.

Johnson, Barbara. *Where Does a Mother Go to Resign?* Minneapolis: Bethany House, 1979, 1994.

Lord, Peter. *Hearing God*. Grand Rapids, MI: Baker Book House, 1988.

_____. *Keeping the Doors Open*. Tarrytown, NY: Fleming H. Revell, 1992.

Lucado, Max. *No Wonder They Call Him the Savior*. Portland: Multnomah Press, 1986.

Mehl, Ron. *God Works the Night Shift*. Sisters, OR: Multnomah Publishers, 1994.

Nori, Don. *No More Sour Grapes*. Shippensburg, PA: Destiny Image Publishers, 1999.

Nouwen, Henri J. M. *The Return of the Prodigal Son*. New York: Doubleday, Image Books, 1992.

Parish, Fawn. *Honor: What Love Looks Like*. Ventura, CA: Regal Books, 1999.

Sheets, Dutch. *Intercessory Prayer*. Ventura, CA: Regal Books, 1996.

Sherrer, Quin. *Good Night, Lord*. Ventura, CA: Regal Books, 2000.

_____. *How to Pray for Your Children*. Ventura, CA: Regal Books, 1998.

_____. *Listen, God Is Speaking to You*. Ann Arbor, MI: Servant Publications, 1999.

_____. *Miracles Happen When You Pray*. Grand Rapids, MI: Zondervan Publishing House, 1997.

Sherrer, Quin, and Ruthanne Garlock. *The Making of a Spiritual Warrior*. Ann Arbor, MI: Servant Publications, 1999.

_____. *Prayers Women Pray*. Ann Arbor, MI: Servant Publications, 1998.

_____. *The Spiritual Warrior's Prayer Guide*. Ann Arbor, MI: Servant Publications, 1992.

_____. *A Woman's Guide to Getting Through Tough Times*. Ann Arbor, MI: Servant Publications, 1998.

_____. *A Woman's Guide to Spiritual Warfare*. Ann Arbor, MI: Servant Publications, 1991.

Towns, Elmer. *Fasting for Spiritual Breakthrough*. Ventura, CA: Regal Books, 1996.

Wagner, C. Peter. *Warfare Prayer*. Ventura, CA: Regal Books, 1992.

Wallis, Arthur. *God's Chosen Fast*. Fort Washington, PA: Christian Literature Crusade, 1968.

White, John. *Parents in Pain*. Downers Grove, IL: InterVarsity Press, 1979.

Yancey, Philip. *What's So Amazing About Grace?* Grand Rapids, MI: Zondervan Publishing House, 1997.

Also by the Authors

By Quin Sherrer

Good Night, Lord
Miracles Happen When You Pray
Listen, God Is Speaking to You

By Quin Sherrer and Ruthanne Garlock

How to Pray for Your Children
How to Forgive Your Children
How to Pray for Your Family and Friends
A Woman's Guide to Spiritual Warfare
The Spiritual Warrior's Prayer Guide
A Woman's Guide to Breaking Bondages
A Woman's Guide to Spirit-Filled Living
A Woman's Guide to Getting Through Tough Times
Prayers Women Pray
Praying Prodigals Home (forthcoming)

By Quin Sherrer and Laura Watson

A Christian Woman's Guide to Hospitality